ANIMALS & INSECTS

ANIMALS & INSECTS

LEARN ABOUT NATURE'S BEASTS

Silver Dolphin

San Diego, California

Silver Dolphin Books
An imprint of the Advantage Publishers Group
5880 Oberlin Drive, San Diego, CA 92121-4794
www.silverdolphinbooks.com

Copyright © Amber Books Ltd 2006

Editorial and design by
Amber Books Ltd
74–77 White Lion Street
London N1 9PF
United Kingdom
www.amberbooks.co.uk

ISBN-13: 978-1-59223-602-2
ISBN-10: 1-59223-602-2

Made in China

1 2 3 4 5 11 10 09 08 07

Author: Paula Hammond
Design: Jerry Williams

All illustrations © IMP AB
Except: 42–43, 64–65, 94–95 (Photos.com); 118–119, 158–159 (U.S. Fish and
Wildlife Services)

Contents

Introduction   6

Ants and Termites   12
Beetles   20
Bugs   32
Wildlife Panorama: Forest Stream   42
Crickets, Mantises, and Cockroaches   44
Flies   52
Moths and Caterpillars   60
Wildlife Panorama: Forest Floor   64
Scorpions   66
Spiders   72
Fleas, Lice, Mites, and Ticks   90
Wildlife Panorama: Tree Stump   94
Wasps and Bees   96
Worms, Leeches, and Slugs   104
Other Creepy Crawlies   110
Wildlife Panorama: Desert Scrub   118
Lizards   120

Snakes   132
Amphibians   150
Wildlife Panorama: Tropical Sea   158
Crustaceans and Mollusks   160
Other Sea Creatures   170

Glossary   190
Index   191

Sticker Fun

Welcome to this exciting and uniquely interactive book. On the pages that follow are fascinating facts about an incredible range of animals, from bloodsucking ticks and mites to giant monitor lizards and deep-sea fish.

You'll also learn all about some unusual creepy-crawly beasts such as frogs, toads, lizards, and snakes, as well as aquatic creatures like sea horses and electric eels. Scattered throughout the book are the yellow "Up Close" pages, which feature detailed looks at some of the more interesting animals.

But this is no ordinary book! To make it even more fun, only the outlines of some creatures are shown, so you get to complete the page by adding the sticker of that animal.

The emperor scorpion sticker from the back of the book fits into the outline on page 68 . . .

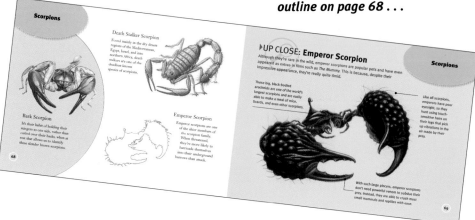

Desert scrub

Out in the hot, dry desert, you might find snakes and scorpions, as well as lizards such as the Salvador's monitor, hunting for their next meal. Complete this desert scene with your animal stickers.

Puss Moth

Death's-head Hawk Moth

Bolas Spider

Australian Redback Spider

Emperor Scorpion

Yellow Fat-tailed Scorpion

Thick-tailed Scorpion

Mole Cricket

Hoverfly

Horsefly

Tsetse Fly

Ornate Mantis

. . . and you can also use it when you create your own desert scene!

At the back of the book you will find 16 pages of stickers. Each scary spider or deadly snake you'll need is labeled, and they all appear in the order they are featured in the book, so you should find it easy to match them up!

Once you've read the book and placed all the stickers in the right places, you can have even more fun with them because they can be used again and again. Throughout the book are five scenes like the one shown above. These show typical landscapes from nature—we've given you two forest scenes, a tree stump, a patch of desert, and a tropical sea scene. Use the stickers to create your own wildlife panorama on each of these scenes. Using what you've learned in this book, you can match the creatures with the environments they live in—or you can create your own imaginative scenes with any stickers you choose!

All About Animals

Whether they fly, swim, crawl, or walk, animals can be found everywhere. No one is sure exactly how many kinds of animals there are, but even ants outnumber us—for every person on earth, there are believed to be at least 1,500 ants! What's more, we know very little about the lives of most of the incredible creatures in our world. Even today there are rain forests, mountains, and icy plains where no human has ever set foot.

Seventy percent of our planet is covered with water, the depths of which are almost entirely unexplored. We know less about the deep ocean than we do about the moon! In fact, we are constantly making new discoveries about our fascinating world and the animals we share it with.

AMAZING CREATURES

On these pages we will be looking up close at some of the planet's most fascinating small animals. For a species to survive, animals need to feed and protect themselves, and to reproduce (many of the strangest animals featured in this book do that very well indeed!).

We all know that poisonous snakes use venom to make a kill, but so too do some types of spiders, lizards, and frogs. Many

Hercules beetle

Jumping spider

European hornet

more examples of nature's weird and wonderful creations: fish that crawl on land, snakes and lizards that fly, and spiders that spend their entire lives in underwater "diving bells"!

After you've completed each page with the correct animal stickers from the back of the book, have fun reusing the stickers to create your own nature scenes on the landscape pages.

species have developed razor-sharp teeth, claws, or stingers to help them survive, but some species have gone a step further. Electric eels hunt by stunning their victims with short bursts of electricity, which they generate inside their own bodies. The viperfish has a glowing "lure" at the end of its long, thin tail, which is used like a fishing rod to help it catch food in the deep, dark oceans. In this book you will find many

Chuckwalla

10

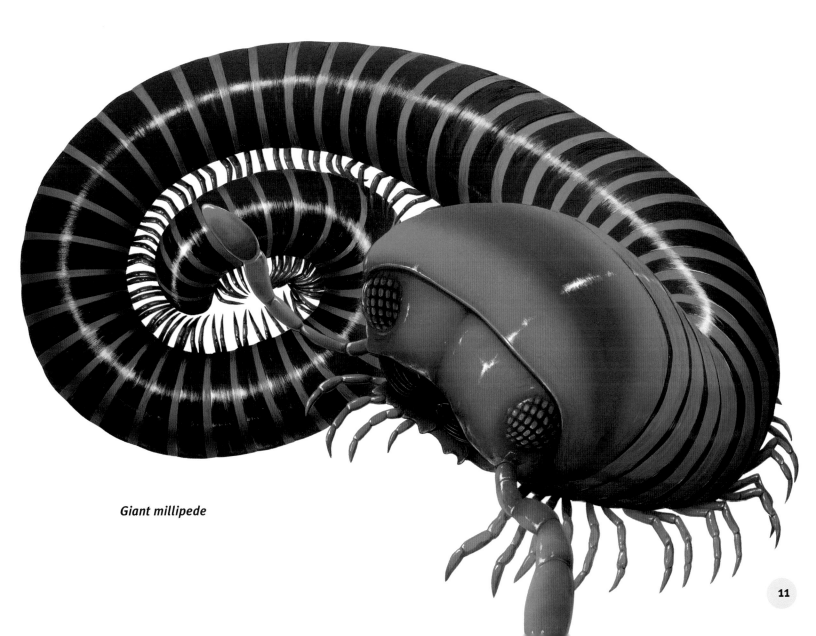

Giant millipede

Ants and Termites

They're so small that it's easy to overlook them. Yet ants are one of our planet's most successful insects. These amazing creatures can be found all over the world, except in the very coldest regions. Like all insects, ants have six legs, and their bodies are divided into three main parts. The first part—the head—contains a pair of long, jointed feelers called antennae. These are used by the ant to touch and sense its surroundings. The middle part of the body is known as the thorax. The rear section is the abdomen. This ends in a bulbous lump that sometimes contains a stinger.

Termites are less widespread than ants and generally only live in warm, damp regions such as Africa. They're often called "white ants," although they're more closely related to cockroaches. What they have in common with ants is that they're "social insects." This means that they live in huge, organized groups called colonies. Ant colonies are usually controlled by a single, oversized queen. All the workers are females. Only at certain times of the year will the queen give birth to males, who die as soon as they have mated. Termite groups are a little more balanced: colonies tend to be shared between a king and queen and can contain both males and females.

12

Ants and Termites

Giant Bulldog Ant

Most ants work together to find food. Giant bulldog ants, however, are badly organized, so they rely on their large size, powerful jaws, and stingers to kill prey.

Did you know?
An ant has two stomachs. One contains food for itself. The other holds "spare" food that it shares with the colony.

Bullet Ant

The bullet ant, found in South America, has a large stinger in its rear. A sting is so painful that people who have been stung say it's like being shot!

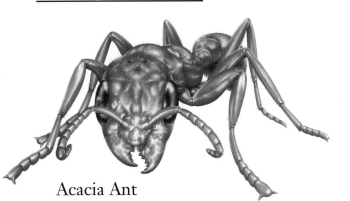

Acacia Ant

For these clever insects, a thorny acacia bush is the ideal home. It's safe, and there's plenty of food. The ants, in return, help keep the bush healthy.

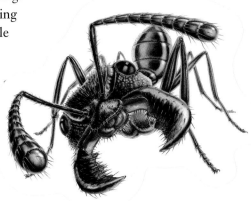

Army Ant

Army ants don't build nests. Instead, they live "on the march" in mobile colonies that contain a queen, her young, the workers, and also the soldiers, who have huge, curved jaws.

Driver Ant

Driver ant colonies, like those of army ants, can contain ten to twenty million workers. These massive groups eat so much that they must be on the move constantly to avoid starvation.

Harvester Ant

Harvester ants collect seeds that the colony's workers reduce to a soft pulp in their jaws. This pulp, called ant bread, is eaten in times of famine.

▶UP CLOSE: **Army Ant**

A column of army ants is a terrifying sight. Instead of having a permanent nest, the whole colony travels together through the rain forest, marching in one long, organized column, like an army.

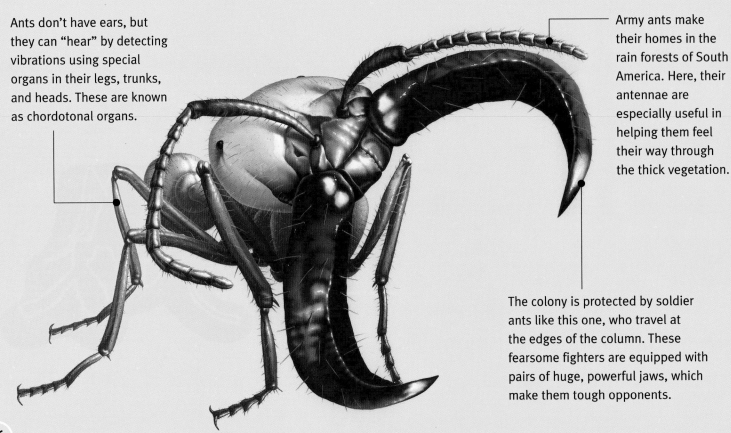

Ants don't have ears, but they can "hear" by detecting vibrations using special organs in their legs, trunks, and heads. These are known as chordotonal organs.

Army ants make their homes in the rain forests of South America. Here, their antennae are especially useful in helping them feel their way through the thick vegetation.

The colony is protected by soldier ants like this one, who travel at the edges of the column. These fearsome fighters are equipped with pairs of huge, powerful jaws, which make them tough opponents.

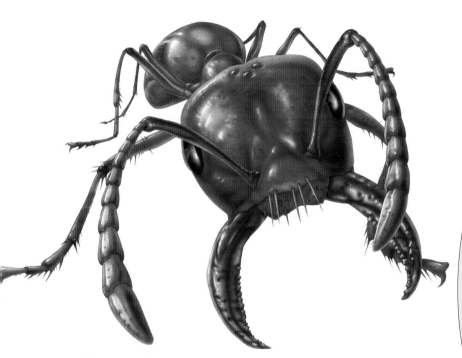

Honeypot Ant

The largest honeypot ant workers turn themselves into living storage containers. When fresh food runs out, other members of the colony "milk" them to feed themselves!

Slave-making Ant

Slave-making ants steal the young (known as pupae) from neighboring ant nests. When the pupae emerge from their cocoons, they believe their captor's colony is their own and begin to work for it.

▶UP CLOSE: Honeypot Ant

Ant colonies are divided into three groups: workers, soldiers, and the queen. These groups look very different. The largest honeypot workers are called "repletes."

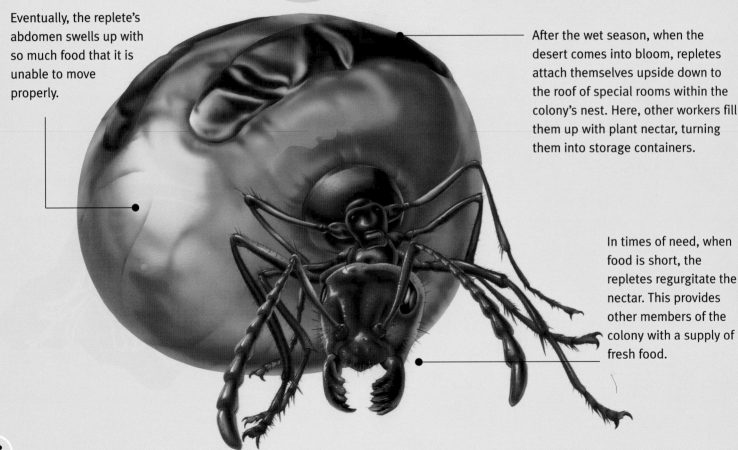

Eventually, the replete's abdomen swells up with so much food that it is unable to move properly.

After the wet season, when the desert comes into bloom, repletes attach themselves upside down to the roof of special rooms within the colony's nest. Here, other workers fill them up with plant nectar, turning them into storage containers.

In times of need, when food is short, the repletes regurgitate the nectar. This provides other members of the colony with a supply of fresh food.

Dry-wood Termite

Dry-wood termites make their nests in dead wood. These nests are often spotted because the termites clean them regularly and leave mounds of waste outside their nests.

Weaver Ant

These skillful insects make their homes in trees. Working as a group, they pull the edges of leaves together and seal them with silk to create strong nests.

Beetles

Beetles are incredible creatures. They're so tough that they're able to live anywhere except in the oceans. In fact, beetles make up a third of all the types of insects in the world.

These fascinating insects vary greatly in size and shape. Some, like ladybugs, are small and almost completely round. Others, like click beetles, are long and flat. However, because they're insects, they all have the same basic design: six legs and a body divided into three segments. Beetles also have two sets of wings. The outer wings are tough and leathery. These aren't used for flying. Instead, they fold down over the beetle's back to cover and protect the other, more fragile flying wings.

Like many insects, beetles change greatly in appearance when they grow into adults. They start life as tiny eggs. These hatch into larvae, which look a little like fat caterpillars. The larvae shed skin as they grow, finally developing into pupae. This is the last stage before the beetles become adults. Strangely, most beetles spend almost their whole lives as larvae. Once they're fully grown, they live only a few months and must find a mate quickly so that the whole wonderful cycle of life can begin again.

Beetles

Bombardier Beetle

Bombardier beetles, like the soldiers they're named after, defend themselves using explosives! When in danger, they can spray blasts of toxic chemicals from their abdomens at their attackers.

Asian Longhorn Beetle

Many people dislike longhorn beetles because they lay their eggs in trees. Once hatched, the caterpillar-like grubs burrow into the trunks, often killing the trees.

Blister Beetle

The 3,000 known species of blister beetles have a unique form of defense. The adults produce an oily fluid that can cause human skin to blister.

Click Beetle

Click beetles have a unique way of getting out of trouble. Thanks to a built-in "catapult," they can propel themselves up to a foot into the air to escape danger.

Dung Beetle

This insect's favorite food is dung! As they prefer to eat in private, they will often form it into a ball and roll it away with their flat heads.

Colorado Beetle

Until farmers arrived in Colorado in the 1850s, this stout yellow insect ate weeds. It now feasts on potatoes and is one of the greatest crop pests.

Beetles

Fog-basking Beetle

When mist creeps across the desert, this little beetle comes out to drink. Raising its abdomen, it collects moisture from the fog, which trickles into its mouthparts.

Elephant Beetle

This mini monster lives in South America's rain forests. Along with the Hercules and Goliath beetles, it has the honor of being one of the world's largest insects.

Giraffe Beetle

Giraffe beetles are found only on the island of Madagascar. These curious insects are actually a type of weevil, which are beetles with an elongated snout.

▶UP CLOSE: **Elephant Beetle**

These South American beetles can grow up to five inches long. It can take up to four years for this giant to grow from a caterpillar-like larvae into this heavily armored, fully formed adult insect.

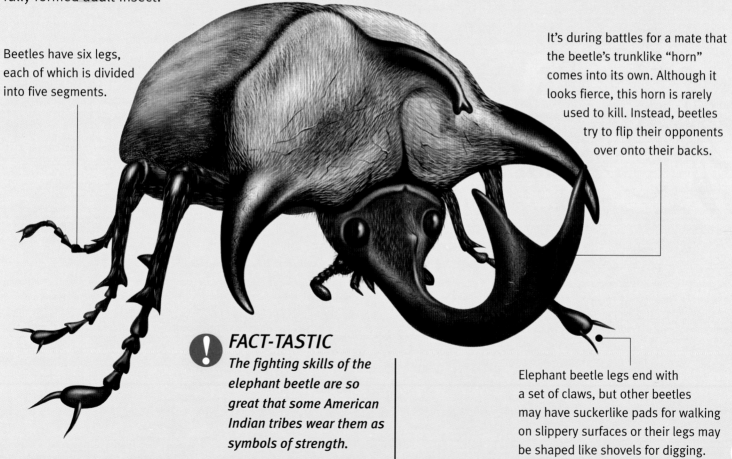

Beetles have six legs, each of which is divided into five segments.

It's during battles for a mate that the beetle's trunklike "horn" comes into its own. Although it looks fierce, this horn is rarely used to kill. Instead, beetles try to flip their opponents over onto their backs.

❗ FACT-TASTIC
The fighting skills of the elephant beetle are so great that some American Indian tribes wear them as symbols of strength.

Elephant beetle legs end with a set of claws, but other beetles may have suckerlike pads for walking on slippery surfaces or their legs may be shaped like shovels for digging.

Beetles

Goliath Beetle

Adult Goliath beetles are one of the world's largest insects. Most of these huge armored beasts can be found in the tropical rain forests of central Africa.

Great Silver Beetle

Silver beetles spend their entire lives in water. While still young (in their larval stage), they feed on tadpoles and water snails, but as adults they're vegetarians.

 FACT-TASTIC

Female beetles may lay a few eggs—or thousands! It all depends on which of the 370,000 species they belong to.

Giant Diving Beetle

These fierce hunters make their homes in still or slow-running water throughout western Europe and parts of Asia. They feed mainly on insects and small fish and frogs.

Harlequin Beetle

An adult harlequin beetle has legs almost as long as its entire body. When threatened, it stands bolt upright. This sudden increase in size scares away most predators!

Did you know?
The rove beetle is also known as the "devil's coach horse." When threatened, it will raise its abdomen and open its jaws like a scorpion!

Hercules Beetle

Male Hercules beetles are olive green with large black spots. Their curved horns can be over three inches long and are used during fights for females.

Rove Beetle

These beetles are found wherever there is rotting matter! They don't feed on this material but instead hunt the grubs and insects that such food attracts.

▶UP CLOSE: **Harlequin Beetle**

This strange-looking beetle lives in South America's tropical forests. Members of this species are also found in the Caribbean, where they're called "jack tree bores" because females lay their eggs in jackfruit trees.

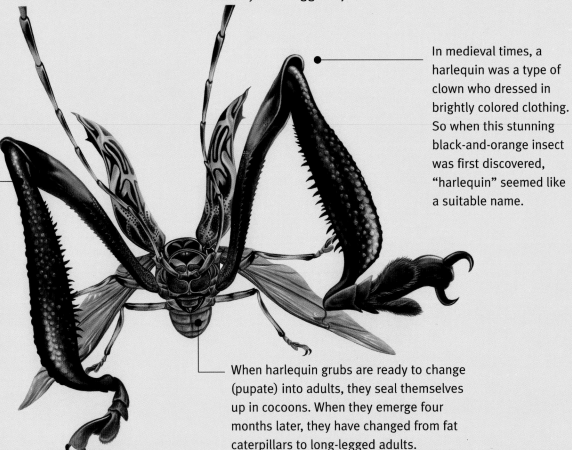

An adult harlequin beetle may grow up to four inches long. Their front legs are even longer— around five inches!

In medieval times, a harlequin was a type of clown who dressed in brightly colored clothing. So when this stunning black-and-orange insect was first discovered, "harlequin" seemed like a suitable name.

When harlequin grubs are ready to change (pupate) into adults, they seal themselves up in cocoons. When they emerge four months later, they have changed from fat caterpillars to long-legged adults.

Sawyer Beetle

Sawyer beetle grubs are real bouncing babies! They spend most of their short, seven-year life as grubs, and as adults they may grow up to 10 inches long.

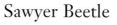

Saber-tooth Ground Beetle

These flat-bodied insects get their strange name from their huge, curved "mandible" jaws. These reminded scientists of the oversized fangs of the prehistoric saber-toothed tiger.

Sexton Beetle

A sexton is someone who digs graves. Sexton beetles have a similar habit. They bury animal corpses, which they feed to their rapidly growing young.

Beetles

Skunk Beetle

Like fog-basking beetles, skunk beetles also perform handstands. However, this has nothing to do with collecting water. It allows them to spray toxic chemicals from their rear ends!

Common Green Tiger Beetle

As you can see, despite the name, common green tiger beetles don't have tiger stripes at all! Rather, the name refers to their skill as hunters.

European Stag Beetle

An adult stag beetle is strikingly attractive, with a pair of purple wing cases and huge, reddish mandibles that stick out like a pair of deer's antlers.

▶UP CLOSE: **European Stag Beetle**

In the animal kingdom, things aren't always what they seem. In the case of the stag beetle, it's the female, with her much smaller jaws, who delivers the most painful bite! The male (pictured) uses his large jaws to compete with other males for mates.

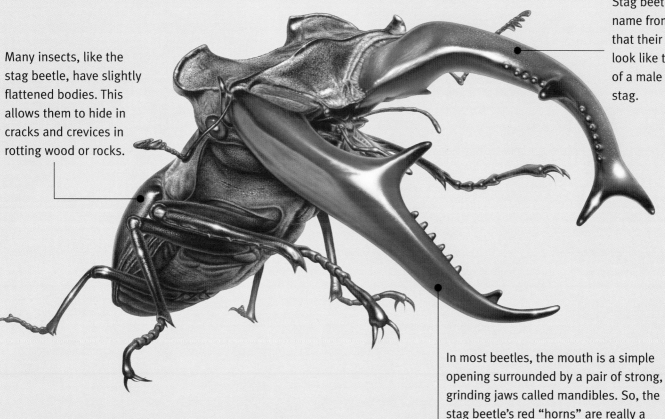

Stag beetles get their name from the fact that their "horns" look like the antlers of a male deer, or stag.

Many insects, like the stag beetle, have slightly flattened bodies. This allows them to hide in cracks and crevices in rotting wood or rocks.

In most beetles, the mouth is a simple opening surrounded by a pair of strong, grinding jaws called mandibles. So, the stag beetle's red "horns" are really a set of extra-large jaws.

Bugs

With over one million species of insects in the world, it isn't always easy to tell one from another. It is possible, however, to sort them into groups based on their similarities. For example, all beetles, no matter what shape or color they are, have a pair of tough wing cases that fold over their fragile flying wings. Bugs have similar identifying features.

There are 82,000 species of bugs. Some of these species have wings, some don't. Some live on land, while some make their homes in water. What they all have in common is the way they eat.

An insect's mouth is usually just a simple opening in its head. Many insects have to cut up leaves or tear flesh to get a meal. For this, an insect has a pair of powerful jaws surrounding its mouth, called mandibles. A bug, however, lives on a liquid diet. Instead of mandibles, it has an elongated mouth called a proboscis. This contains sharp "needles" known as stylets. The stylets can be stuck into plants or animals, allowing the bug to suck up a meal of sap or blood. This is why bedbugs, which feed on humans in this way, are such unpopular and unwelcome household guests!

Bugs

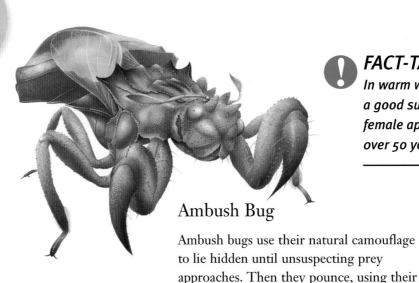

❗ FACT-TASTIC
In warm weather and with a good supply of food, a female aphid can produce over 50 young each week.

Bedbug

Of the 90 known species of bedbugs, only three feed on humans. As they eat, their soft bodies swell up and turn purple with the intake of blood.

Ambush Bug

Ambush bugs use their natural camouflage to lie hidden until unsuspecting prey approaches. Then they pounce, using their large front legs to hold their victims tight.

Common Aphid

Aphids produce a sweet liquid called honeydew. This is supposed to deter predators, but some species of ants find it so delicious that they "farm" these little insects!

Bee Assassin Bug

These fearsome-looking bugs are specialist bee hunters. To reduce the risk of being injured during the kill, they inject the bees with venom, which quickly disables them.

Chagas Bug

These tiny bloodsucking insects come out at night to eat. They're often called "kissing bugs" because they usually feed on the soft skin around their victims' mouths.

Butterfly Bug

This butterfly bug is in its young, or nymph, form. The tuft of long streamers in its rear helps it to hide among the moss on tree branches.

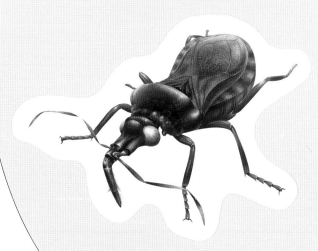

Bugs

Cicada

Cicadas are famous for their loud chirrups, which they use to defend territory and attract a mate. This "song" can be heard over a third of a mile away!

Firefly

There are approximately 2,000 species of fireflies, which are also called lightning bugs.

❗ FACT-TASTIC

Young cicadas spend the majority of their lives underground. This can be as long as 17 years!

Damsel Bug

Damsel bugs feed mainly on soft-bodied insects such as aphids. Yet, if food is scarce, they are perfectly happy to eat members of their own species, too.

▶UP CLOSE: **Firefly**

These popular insects are known by a number of different names throughout the world, including lightning bugs, glow flies, and glowworms.

In some species of fireflies, the females have no wings, so they must watch the male's flashing display from nearby foliage and then signal their approval with flashes of their own.

The same chemicals that produce the dramatic light shows also make the fireflies taste terrible. This helps to protect them from predators.

During the mating season, this spectacular insect uses a special organ in its abdomen to make dramatic light displays in the night sky. The brightness, speed, and complexity of the male's display helps him attract a mate.

Bugs

Fungus Bug

Fungus bugs are easily recognized by their flat bodies, which look a bit like tree bark. Their shape allows them to squeeze into narrow cracks in decaying wood where their favorite food—fungus—grows.

Lantern Bug

Chinese lantern bugs are also known as peanut-headed or alligator bugs. They are recognized by the long and brightly colored growths on top of their heads.

Pond Skater

When you're as small and light as a pond skater, the surface of water can hold your weight. A pond skater pushes itself across water using this surface tension.

▶UP CLOSE: **Lantern Bug**

To protect themselves, some harmless animals imitate more dangerous species, either by mimicking their color scheme (red and yellow often means danger in the natural world) or by pretending to have big, scary eyes, like the lantern bug.

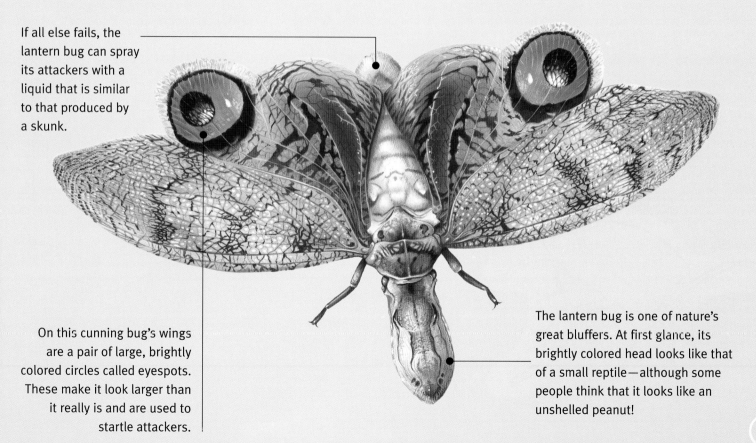

If all else fails, the lantern bug can spray its attackers with a liquid that is similar to that produced by a skunk.

On this cunning bug's wings are a pair of large, brightly colored circles called eyespots. These make it look larger than it really is and are used to startle attackers.

The lantern bug is one of nature's great bluffers. At first glance, its brightly colored head looks like that of a small reptile—although some people think that it looks like an unshelled peanut!

Bugs

Spittle Bug

These little bugs hide themselves using bubbles of foamy liquid that they produce from their anus and fill with air by bobbing their bodies up and down.

FACT-TASTIC

Spittle bugs are common worldwide and are also known as froghoppers. The foamy liquid they produce is known as "cuckoo spit."

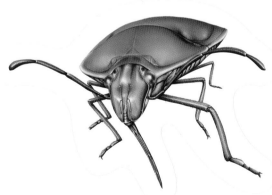

Stinkbug

As their name suggests, stinkbugs produce foul smells to chase away attackers! This terrible odor comes from special glands on the side of the thorax.

Toad Bug

Like toads, these flat, squat bugs have broad bodies and large, bulging eyes on the side of their heads. They even hop rather than fly!

Toe Biter

Toe biters are really a type of giant water bug. Their front legs are designed to grab prey, and they'll quickly seize anything that enters the water—hence the name.

Treehopper

When feeding, groups of treehoppers gather together on a branch, all facing the same way, to give the impression that they are spines on the plant.

Forest stream

Along a forest stream like this, you might find animals that like damp conditions, including frogs, toads, leeches, and water beetles. Complete this forest stream scene with your animal stickers.

Crickets, Mantises, and Cockroaches

Scientists discover around 10,000 new insect species every year, but most of us will encounter only a small percentage of these weird and wonderful creatures. That's not because they're rare, but because they're experts at keeping themselves well out of sight. After all, when you're small, being able to hide from animals that want to eat you is a very handy trick!

Stick insects are the masters of hiding. These slim-bodied little insects stay out of sight by looking like leaves and twigs. Many of them are plain brown or green, but those that make their homes in tropical forests are multicolored, with spikes and thorns over their bodies to help them blend in with the vegetation.

Crickets, grasshoppers, and locusts, which are closely related to stick insects, have less elaborate camouflage. However, it's just as effective. These little jumping insects are usually so difficult to spot that often only their high-pitched "song" can be heard. Even the lowly cockroach—which is a distant relative of the praying mantis—manages to keep itself well out of view most of the time. When they are seen, however, beware—these common household pests usually come in huge numbers!

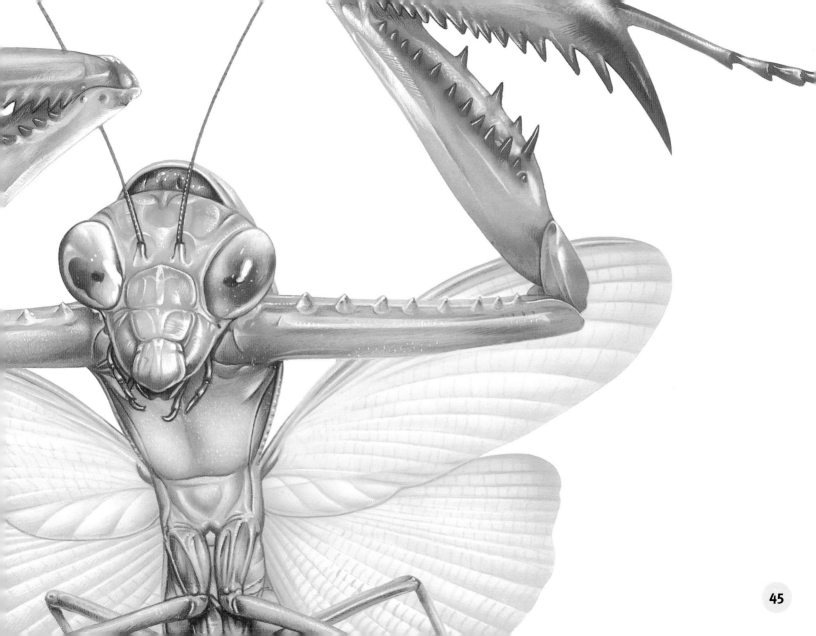

Armored Ground Cricket

Young ground crickets can't fly, but this doesn't stop swarms of them from wiping out crops as they march across the African savanna in search of a meal.

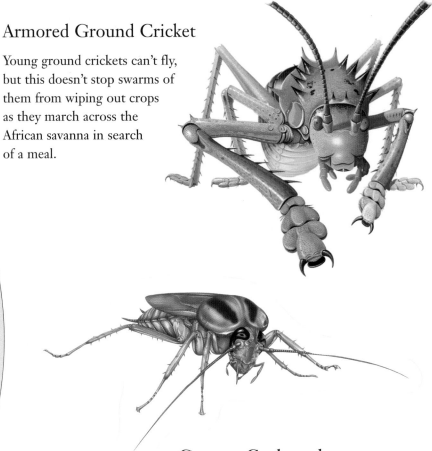

African Desert Locust

These little grasshoppers have huge appetites. A swarm of locusts, which can contain 150 billion insects, can munch its way through 100,000 tons of food a day!

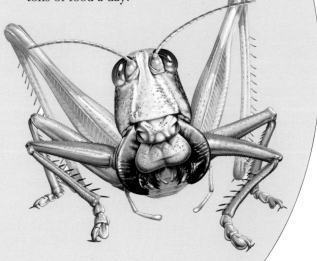

German Cockroach

It's the German cockroach that has given other species of roaches such a bad name. Because the females breed continuously, groups of these pests can quickly reach plague numbers.

▶UP CLOSE: German Cockroach

German cockroaches make their homes in our homes. In fact, these little pests can't survive in areas without humans. That's probably because they've come to rely on us for their food!

Many species of cockroaches can't fly. Instead, they each have six powerful legs and can run at incredible speeds. In fact, they're the world's fastest insects.

There are around 4,000 known species of cockroaches. The most common—and the one that we are most likely to see—is the German cockroach. It is usually pale brown in color.

Unlike other insects such as ants and beetles, a cockroach's antennae are incredibly long. These sensitive feelers are believed to be able to help the roach scent out food.

! FACT-TASTIC
The remarkable sound produced by hissing cockroaches is so loud that it can be heard up to 12 feet away.

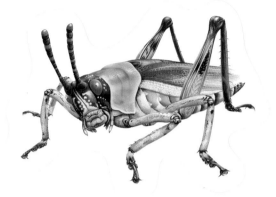

Elegant Grasshopper

This widespread species is named for its brightly colored body. It may look attractive, but it's actually designed as a warning to predators to stay well away.

Giant Weta

Not all wetas are giants. The name refers to the species, regardless of its size. Most wetas are now threatened with extinction in their native New Zealand.

Florida Walking-stick

These insects are examples of natural camouflage at work. Their long, thin bodies look like twigs. This allows them to blend completely with their surroundings.

Did you know?
The name "weta" comes from a native Maori word, wetapunga, which means, perhaps a little unfairly, "god of ugly things"!

Madagascar Hissing Cockroach

On every segment of this giant insect's body are openings known as spiracles. When threatened by predators, the cockroach squeezes air out of these holes to make its loud trademark hiss.

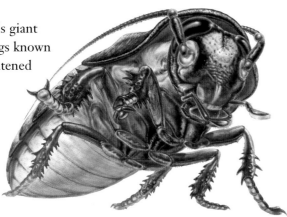

Mole Cricket

These brownish insects have many features in common with real moles, including a layer of fine hair over their bodies that gives them a velvety appearance.

MacLeay's Specter

These Australian stick insects get their curious name from the way they use their natural camouflage to appear and disappear—in a "ghostlike" way—among the vegetation.

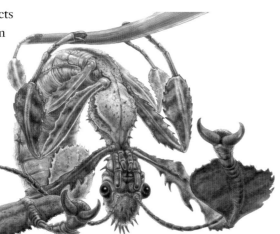

▶UP CLOSE: **MacLeay's Specter**

MacLeay's specter eggs contain food that ants find irresistible. The ants carry them to their nests, eat the food, and discard the rest. The discarded eggs hatch inside the ant's nest, where they're safe from predators.

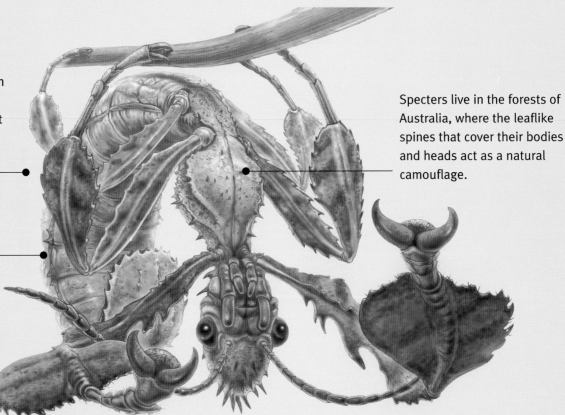

MacLeay's specters are stick insects. These amazing creatures mimic the vegetation around them. If they sit completely still, they're almost impossible to spot among the vegetation.

Specters live in the forests of Australia, where the leaflike spines that cover their bodies and heads act as a natural camouflage.

When young specter nymphs hatch, they look and behave just like ants. Once out of the ant's nest, however, they molt into the more familiar adult form.

Ornate Mantis

Mantises have excellent eyesight and can turn their heads around to look behind themselves without moving. This skill allows them to track their prey without giving away their position.

Common Praying Mantis

These odd-looking insects are the favorite food of several species of birds and bats. That's why they rely on their natural camouflage to blend in with their surroundings.

Predatory Bush Cricket

Predatory bush crickets are among Europe's largest insects. These creatures can be found on warm, dry grasslands throughout Mediterranean Europe, northern and sub-Saharan Africa, and Australia.

! FACT-TASTIC

Praying mantises get their unusual name from the way they hold their spiked forelegs at rest, which resembles praying.

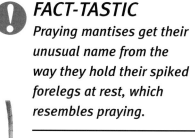

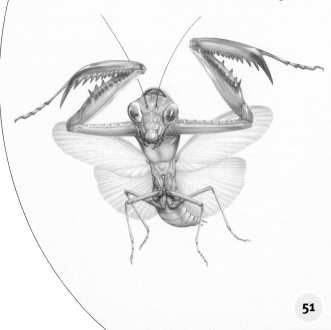

Flies

Not all insects that fly can be called "flies." Only those with one pair of well-developed wings are true flies.

Throughout the world there are around 122,000 different species of flies. This enormous list includes many names with which we're very familiar, such as bluebottles, crane flies, and mosquitoes. Some of these are true mini monsters, capable of transmitting deadly diseases such as malaria and sleeping sickness. This happens due to the way they eat. Flies don't actually bite—in fact, they can't open their jaws, but they do have needle-sharp mouthparts that can pierce the skin. Flies that feed on blood, like mosquitoes, inject saliva into these wounds to keep the victim's blood from clotting while they drink. It's this saliva that carries disease.

Luckily, not all flies are harmful. Some are gardeners that help flowers grow by carrying pollen from plant to plant. Others are pest controllers, eating those insects that would cause us problems if they were allowed to spread unchecked. Some even help us dispose of our waste by feeding it to their young! They may often be a nuisance, but in the insect world, every creature has an important job to do—and this includes flies.

Flies

Black Fly

Some African and American species of these stout, humpbacked flies carry the larvae of roundworms. If they infect a human, they can cause blindness.

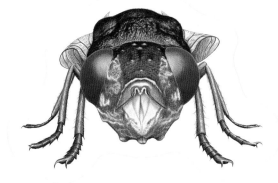

Did you know?
Fly young are often called maggots. These eating machines spend their entire time feeding, storing enough energy to change into adults.

Botfly

These large, bluish insects are parasites that live and feed off (or in) the bodies of other animals. Not surprisingly, this is usually harmful to the unwilling host.

Bluebottle

Bluebottles lay their eggs on rotten meat (including corpses), human excrement, and occasionally even live animals. This unappetizing mix provides food for the young maggots!

Dance Fly

All members of this family of predatory insects perform elaborate acrobatics during the mating season. Others present their mate-to-be with gifts such as dead insects wrapped in leaves.

! FACT-TASTIC
The buzzing you hear when houseflies are nearby is the sound of their wings beating 200 times a minute.

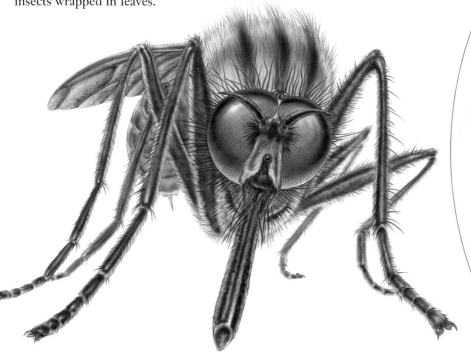

Horsefly

These fat, hairless insects are easy to recognize thanks to their large, colorful eyes. Horseflies are a widespread species and are also known as gadflies and deerflies.

▶UP CLOSE: **Dance Fly**

Dance flies belong to a large group that contains around 3,500 known species. These acrobatic insects can be found all over the world, except in the Arctic and Antarctic.

Between the eyes, near the middle of the head, are a pair of antennae. These sensitive feelers can detect changes in the surrounding air; this is how the fly knows when danger is near.

The fly's thin wings are laced with tiny veins. These veins not only carry blood to the wings but also help to keep the wings stiff during flight.

! *FACT-TASTIC*
Flies generally prefer warm weather. Most species will die if the temperature starts to drop unexpectedly, although a few hibernate.

Two large eyes cover most of the fly's head. These compound eyes are made up of thousands of six-sided lenses, each of which shows part of the whole image.

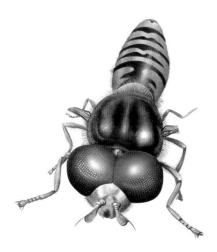

Hoverfly

It's easy to confuse a hoverfly with a bee or wasp, because many species have yellow-and-black-striped abdomens. Their wings also make a characteristically loud droning sound.

Malarial Mosquito

Mosquito is a Spanish word that means "little fly," which is exactly what mosquitoes are. Only females drink blood and pass on diseases—males feed on nectar.

Louse

These widespread parasites come equipped with everything they need to make a meal of their hosts, including sharp and strong clawed feet for grasping hair and feathers.

Flies

Screwworm Fly

An invasion of screwworms can mean ruin for any farmer. These insects lay eggs in open wounds on animals, and the eggs hatch into maggots like this one. Any animal is a target, but newborn cattle are especially vulnerable.

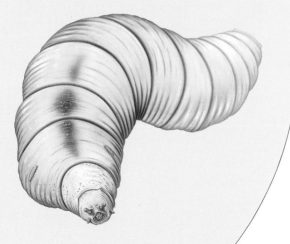

Robber Fly

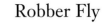

These "thieves" prey on many different kinds of insects, plucking their prey out of the air and quickly paralyzing it with toxic chemicals.

Tsetse Fly

All but three species of these gray-brown insects carry the parasites that cause sleeping sickness. Because of this, attempts are being made to wipe them out in Africa.

►UP CLOSE: **Malarial Mosquito**

There are around 3,100 known species of mosquitoes, but it's the one that carries malaria—and a host of other diseases—that is the most dangerous to humans.

These short antennae act as the insect's feelers. Usually, the antennae of the females have a slightly feathery appearance.

These delicate little flies can be brightly colored, especially those that live in tropical countries. However, in most species, their abdomens and legs are covered in white, brown, and black bands.

❗ FACT-TASTIC
The high-pitched buzzing noise made by mosquitoes is actually the sound of their wings flapping at about 1,000 times a second.

Female malarial mosquitoes feed on blood by inserting their sharp snout into the victim's skin, like a syringe. They then inject saliva into the open wound to keep the blood from congealing.

Moths and Caterpillars

These fragile-looking creatures are among some of the most beautiful members of the insect family.

With their occasionally unusual colors and slender bodies, moths are popular visitors in gardens and parks all over the world. But how do you tell the difference between a moth and a butterfly? Scientifically speaking, there's very little difference at all. Worldwide, there are around 165,000 species of moths and butterflies, with new ones being discovered all the time. These exquisite insects belong to a group known as lepidopterans. Most scientific names are based on either Greek or Latin words, and in Greek, *lepidoptera* means "scale wing." This refers to the delicate scales that can be found on the wings of both moths and butterflies.

The larvae of all butterflies and moths are called caterpillars. These long-bodied eating machines munch their way through as many leaves as they can, growing larger and larger while trying to avoid birds and other predators. Then they form a hard shell around themselves, known as a pupa or chrysalis, in which their bodies transform into a completely different shape—an adult moth or butterfly.

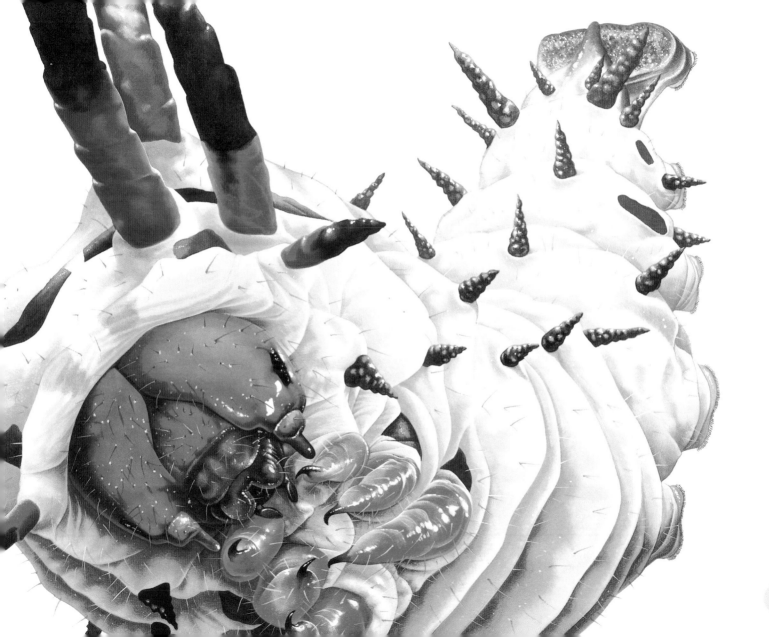

Moths and Caterpillars

Death's-head Hawk Moth

It's the famous "death's head" skull pattern that gives these large moths such a bad reputation. In the Middle Ages, they were believed to bring bad luck to those who saw them.

Hickory Horned Devil

These huge, spiky green caterpillars are the larvae of the regal moth. Spikes and ten reddish-orange horns provide them with much-needed protection from predators.

Did you know?
The world's largest butterfly is probably the Queen Alexandra's birdwing from New Guinea. It has an 11-inch wingspan.

Tiger Moth

This moth's brightly colored body is a warning to stay away! When young, the moth larvae feed on toxic plants and absorb the poisons, which makes them poisonous themselves.

Lobster Moth

When they hatch, lobster moths look like ants. As they grow into adults, they turn red and develop enlarged, lobsterlike tails, which they use to scare away predators.

! FACT-TASTIC

The ancient Greeks believed that when they died, their souls left their bodies and took the form of butterflies.

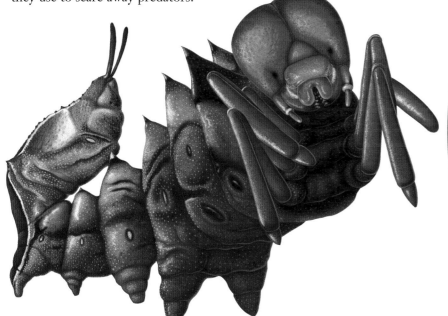

Puss Moth

Puss moth larvae are slow-moving and easy to catch, so they use their large false eyespots and their bright red heads to scare away hunters.

Forest floor

On the forest floor, you might find woodland insects: beetles, ants, and millipedes among the dead leaves, and caterpillars munching in the branches. Complete this forest floor scene with your animal stickers.

Scorpions

Scorpions have been around for a very long time. Fossils of these hardy little creatures have been found dating back almost 400 million years. That's around 160 million years before the arrival of the dinosaurs!

These ancient creatures aren't insects but arachnids. That's the same group to which spiders belong. Like all arachnids, scorpions are quite small, with a body divided into two main parts. The front part is called the cephalothorax. This includes the head and thorax. The rear end is the abdomen. Because they're arachnids, not insects, scorpions also have eight legs, rather than the six of insects.

Despite their small size, almost all arachnids are powerful predators—and scorpions are no exception. These fearsome little hunters come equipped with a pair of powerful, crushing claws and a long, jointed tail. This tail can be arched over the scorpion's body to deliver a powerful sting. Most arachnids carry some type of poison, but scorpions have a particularly dangerous blend in their stingers. Although scorpions will only sting to protect themselves, 25 of the world's 1,400 known species are capable of killing humans. Luckily, most scorpions prefer to avoid us, spending their days hidden under rocks or beneath leaves.

Scorpions

Death Stalker Scorpion

Found mainly in the dry desert regions of the Mediterranean, Egypt, Israel, and into northern Africa, death stalkers are one of the deadliest known species of scorpions.

Bark Scorpion

It's their habit of holding their stingers to one side, rather than curled over their backs, when at rest that allows us to identify these slender brown scorpions.

Emperor Scorpion

Emperor scorpions are one of the shier members of the scorpion family. When threatened, they're more likely to barricade themselves into their underground burrows than attack.

▶UP CLOSE: **Emperor Scorpion**

Although they're rare in the wild, emperor scorpions are popular pets and have even appeared as extras in films such as *The Mummy*. This is because, despite their impressive appearance, they're really quite timid.

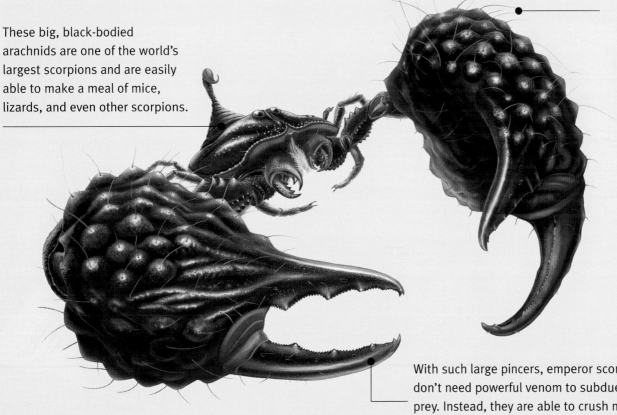

These big, black-bodied arachnids are one of the world's largest scorpions and are easily able to make a meal of mice, lizards, and even other scorpions.

Like all scorpions, emperors have poor eyesight, so they hunt using touch-sensitive hairs on their legs that pick up vibrations in the air made by their prey.

With such large pincers, emperor scorpions don't need powerful venom to subdue their prey. Instead, they are able to crush most small mammals and reptiles with ease.

Scorpions

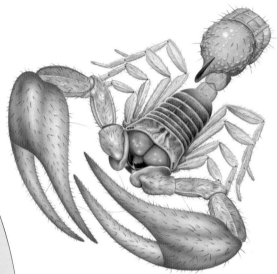

Old World Scorpion

These pale-bodied arachnids are among some of the deadliest members of the scorpion family. Unless medical help can be found immediately, their sting is frequently fatal to humans.

Thick-tailed Scorpion

Like all arachnids, these powerful little hunters are small but deadly. This lethal species feeds on insects, mice, and lizards, which they dissect with their powerful pincers.

Yellow Fat-tailed Scorpion

Yellow scorpion venom is held in two glands that are located just below the stinger. It's these especially large glands that make their tails look so fat.

▶UP CLOSE: **Thick-tailed Scorpion**

There are more than 500 different species of thick-tailed scorpions around the world. Some have the ability to spray venom from their tail up to three feet!

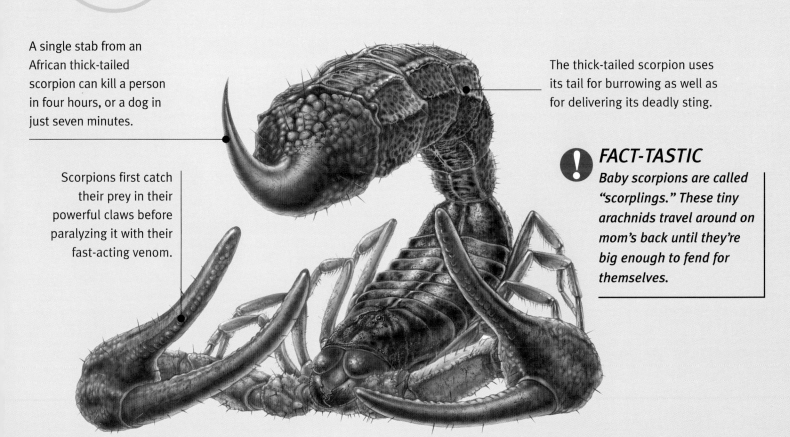

A single stab from an African thick-tailed scorpion can kill a person in four hours, or a dog in just seven minutes.

The thick-tailed scorpion uses its tail for burrowing as well as for delivering its deadly sting.

Scorpions first catch their prey in their powerful claws before paralyzing it with their fast-acting venom.

❗ FACT-TASTIC
Baby scorpions are called "scorplings." These tiny arachnids travel around on mom's back until they're big enough to fend for themselves.

Spiders

Say the word "spider" and many people will shudder. These small creatures are one of the world's most dreaded animals. There's even a term for the fear of spiders: arachnophobia. Worldwide, about one in every three people admit that they are afraid of spiders. This is a shame, because spiders can be found almost everywhere!

Spiders belong to a widespread group of animals called arachnids. Unlike insects, which have six legs (three sets of two), arachnids have eight legs (four sets of two), no wings, and no antennae.

Spiders are classified according to whether or not they build webs and what type of webs they build. All spiders produce silk, but some are hunters who don't make webs. Others, like black widows, trap their prey in elaborate "tangle webs," while orb weavers create round webs that look like the spokes of a wheel.

Whether they are hunters or web builders, spiders come in an amazing range of colors and sizes—from almost microscopic black comb-footed spiders to the South American red-kneed tarantulas, which can grow up to 10 inches across.

Spiders

FACT-TASTIC

Spider silk is an amazingly strong natural fiber. In the South Pacific, islanders use Nephila spider silk to make fishing nets.

Ant Mimic Spider

Why would a spider want to look like an ant? Spiders mimic many insects, but ants are useful to imitate because they're often toxic and avoided by predators.

Australian Redback Spider

Australian redbacks—or jockey spiders, as they are also called—are a secretive species. These poisonous spiders hide themselves away in shady corners, making them hard to spot!

Bird-eating Spider

Despite their name, these South American spiders are more likely to make a meal of mice or small lizards, although they have been known to take small birds from their nests.

Did you know?
Some baby spiderlings parachute by releasing strands of silk from their abdomens and waiting for the wind to catch them.

Black Widow Spider

Black widow spiders deserve their bad reputation. After mating, the female often eats the much smaller male, which is how these "widows" earned their rather grisly name.

Bolas Spider

When a meal is in sight, bolas spiders swirl a sticky, silken thread around their heads and, with perfect timing, release it to hit their prey.

Brazilian Wandering Spider

These fast, aggressive spiders live in tropical rain forests, but they like to travel! They have even made it as far as Europe by stowing away on cargo ships.

Spiders

African Cave Spider

These shy spiders are genuine living fossils—their ancestors date back to the time before the African and American landmasses separated. This is why similar species are also found in South America.

Central American Wandering Spider

Most spiders either build webs to trap their prey or hunt them down. Wandering spiders are hunters, which means they are fast, strong, and have excellent eyesight.

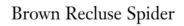

Brown Recluse Spider

These highly dangerous spiders are relatively easy to identify because they have six eyes, arranged in pairs on their heads. Most other North American spiders have eight eyes.

Crab Spider

These skilled ambushers spend their time hidden in leaves or flowers, waiting for prey. They can even change their skin color to blend in with their surroundings.

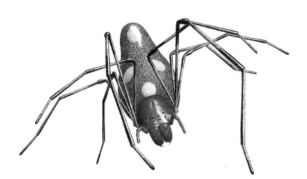

Dwarf Spider

In Britain, dwarf spiders are commonly called money spiders because they are believed to be lucky. These tiny arachnids are mainly found in fields and open grasslands.

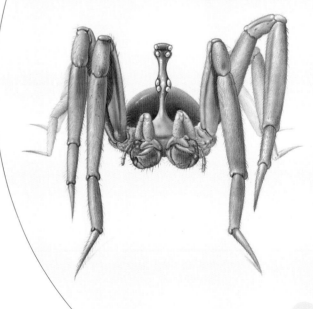

Dewdrop Spider

Dewdrops have an unusual lifestyle, a bit like that of a cuckoo. They live with—and steal food from—other species. They are usually found in the webs of other spiders.

▶UP CLOSE: **Crab Spider**

These slow-moving arachnids come in such a wide variety of colors that it can be difficult even for experts to identify them correctly!

❗ FACT-TASTIC

Spiders don't have any muscles in their legs. It's the blood pressure in their bodies that allows them to extend their legs.

The crab spider's front pair of legs are longer than the other six. These are kept spread apart, ready to close in quickly on any prey that may pass by. Bees, butterflies, and other spiders are favorite meals.

Once hidden in vegetation, crab spiders anchor themselves in place, using their four back legs to get a good grip. When walking, they move like a crab, using scuttling, sideways movements.

Small, hollow fangs are used to inject a powerful paralyzing venom. This means that the spider's victims can be immobilized without the need for a web.

European Raft Spider

These fishing spiders hunt by stretching out their long legs over the water's surface to feel for the tiny vibrations that are made by approaching prey.

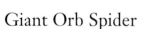 **FACT-TASTIC**

A male orb spider is much smaller than a female and can live in her web— and even mate with her unnoticed!

Giant Orb Spider

Orb spiders make the largest and strongest of all known spider webs. Some of these spectacular golden traps are 20 feet high and seven feet wide.

Horned Orb Weaver

These tropical spiders build large, round webs between the branches of trees to catch flying insects. These webs are so strong, they have been known to trap small birds!

Spiders

Common House Spider

Fine webs in the corner of a room mean that a house spider is on the prowl. These triangular constructions trap prey by tangling them in silken threads.

Jumping Spider

Jumping spiders pounce on their prey. They're able to do this because, compared to many other spiders, they have superb eyesight, which helps them judge distances well.

! FACT-TASTIC

Some spiders can jump up to 40 times their own body length. Lynx spiders often leap into the air to catch flying insects.

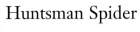

Huntsman Spider

Huntsman spiders are named for their skills at hunting down prey. These nocturnal spiders are extremely agile and powerful predators.

Australian Mouse Spider

There are eight known species of mouse spiders found in Australia. These widespread arachnids are often confused with funnel-web spiders, and both species are highly toxic.

Ogre-faced Spider

These slender spiders have eight eyes, two of which point forward like giant searchlights. These eyes not only give them excellent vision but also a startling appearance!

Green Lynx Spider

These spiders get their name from the catlike way in which they pounce on prey. They prefer to lie in wait for prey, hiding themselves in vegetation and waiting for the right moment to strike.

▶UP CLOSE: **Ogre-faced Spider**

By day, these long-legged hunters remain hidden among the vegetation. Once night falls, however, they emerge to hunt, hanging upside down close to the ground from a strand of silk.

Ogre-faced spiders have eight eyes. Two of these are huge and face forward, which gives them excellent vision. This is especially important when these spiders hunt at night.

Ogre-faced spiders get their scientific name *(Deinopis)* from the Greek words *deinos,* which means "fearful," and *opis,* for "appearance."

These spiders don't build webs but instead make small nets. When hunting, they hold these nets in front of them, grasped in their forelegs. Then they wait, ready to drop their nets on any prey that passes close by.

❗ FACT-TASTIC
The weight of insects eaten by spiders every year is more than the total weight of the entire human population!

Pirate Spider

There are around 200 species of pirate spiders. These yellow-brown arachnids are also called cannibal spiders thanks to their preference for eating members of their own species!

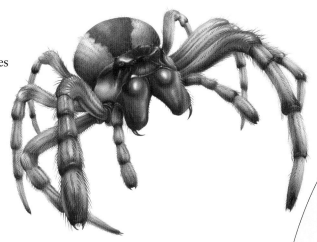

Portia Spider

A Portia's main diet is other spiders. They prey on species from up to 11 different families and, for each species, a different hunting technique is used.

Purse-web Spider

Inside their underground burrows, purse-web spiders hang upside down, waiting for a meal. These secretive spiders are almost blind but detect prey with touch-sensitive hairs on their legs.

Spiders

King Baboon Spider

These large, rusty red spiders are notoriously bad tempered and will rear up on their back legs to display their large fangs when they're threatened or annoyed.

Mexican Red-kneed Spider

Mexico's red-kneed spiders are more commonly known as tarantulas. These large, hairy hunting spiders have become so popular as pets that they are now rare in the wild.

Spitting Spider

Spitting spiders have a unique way of hunting. Their silk glands are connected to their poison sacs, which allows them to spray their prey with venomous silk.

▶UP CLOSE: **Mexican Red-kneed Spider**

Mexican red-kneed spiders are one of the most easily recognized species of tarantulas—which is a name given to any large, hairy tropical spider.

When spiders walk, they move the first and third legs on one side of the body at the same time as the second and fourth legs on the other side.

These Mexican monsters are generally harmless to humans. However, they should only be handled by experts, as they shed tiny hairs that can cause a burning sensation, rashes, and even blindness.

Spiders inject their prey with special chemicals, or enzymes, that dissolve flesh into a liquid. This liquid can then be sucked up through a short, strawlike opening around the spider's mouth.

85

Spiders

Indian Tiger Spider

Young tiger spiderlings often hunt together in packs. Once the food starts to run out, however, they're happy to make a meal of their brothers and sisters!

FACT-TASTIC

Many spiders live for only a year, but some female tarantulas have been known to live for 20 years in captivity.

Sydney Funnel-web Spider

These large, blue-black arachnids typically make their homes in any damp crack or rock crevice. Here they build a thick, tubular web and sit in wait for prey.

Did you know?
Funnel-web spiders cannot be killed by pouring boiling water down their holes or spraying them with insecticide. They need to be dug up one by one!

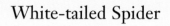

Trapdoor Spider

This cunning arachnid lives in a burrow. At the entrance is a hidden outer "trapdoor" hinged with silk. Here, the spider lies in wait until prey approaches.

White-tailed Spider

Just one bite from this mouse-gray Australian spider can cause horrific wounds. This is because its venom causes an allergic reaction that makes skin burn and blister.

Water Spider

Many spiders live and hunt on the water's edge, but this amazing species spends almost its entire life submerged in an underwater "diving bell" made of silk.

▶UP CLOSE: **Trapdoor Spider**

Trapdoor spiders are an extremely adaptable species that make their homes in rain forests, on grasslands, and in dry desert regions.

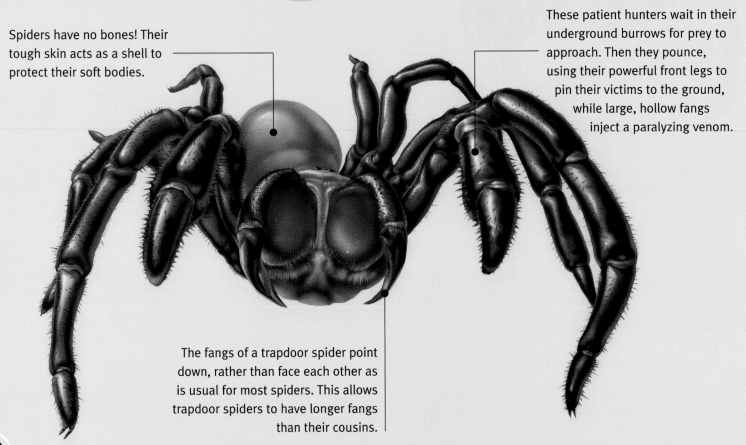

Spiders have no bones! Their tough skin acts as a shell to protect their soft bodies.

These patient hunters wait in their underground burrows for prey to approach. Then they pounce, using their powerful front legs to pin their victims to the ground, while large, hollow fangs inject a paralyzing venom.

The fangs of a trapdoor spider point down, rather than face each other as is usual for most spiders. This allows trapdoor spiders to have longer fangs than their cousins.

Wolf Spider

Wolf spiders don't make webs. Instead, they stalk their prey and, when it's within reach, pounce. Their silk is used to make egg sacs.

Yellow Sac Spider

Sac spiders hide out during the day in thin, paperlike sacs of silk. These refuges can often be found in gardens or homes, especially in out-of-the-way spots.

! FACT-TASTIC
It's believed that yellow sac spiders may be responsible for more bites on humans than any other species of spider.

Wood Louse Spider

As you might expect, these small, reddish spiders hunt wood lice. They're most active at night, but, even during the day, they're so aggressive that they'll bite anything or anyone that disturbs them.

Fleas, Lice, Mites, and Ticks

Fleas and lice have six legs, plus a pair of antennae, which tells us that they're insects. Mites and ticks have eight legs, which means they're arachnids. Despite these differences, all these beasts have one thing in common: they're parasites.

It's easy to be impressed by fearsome hunters such as lions, but parasites are some of the world's most successful killers. A parasite is an animal that lives on (or in) the body of another animal—even humans. The reason they're so deadly is that many of them feed on blood. So, as they move from host to host, they pass infections directly into the host's bloodstream. Even relatively harmless dust mites leave behind droppings that can cause asthma and other dangerous allergies.

The problem is that these microscopic monsters are so common it's difficult to avoid them. Head lice are passed from person to person very easily. And don't believe the rumor that only dirty people get infected. Lice, like most parasites, will make a meal of any passing animal, and they actually prefer clean hair, which is easier to move around in!

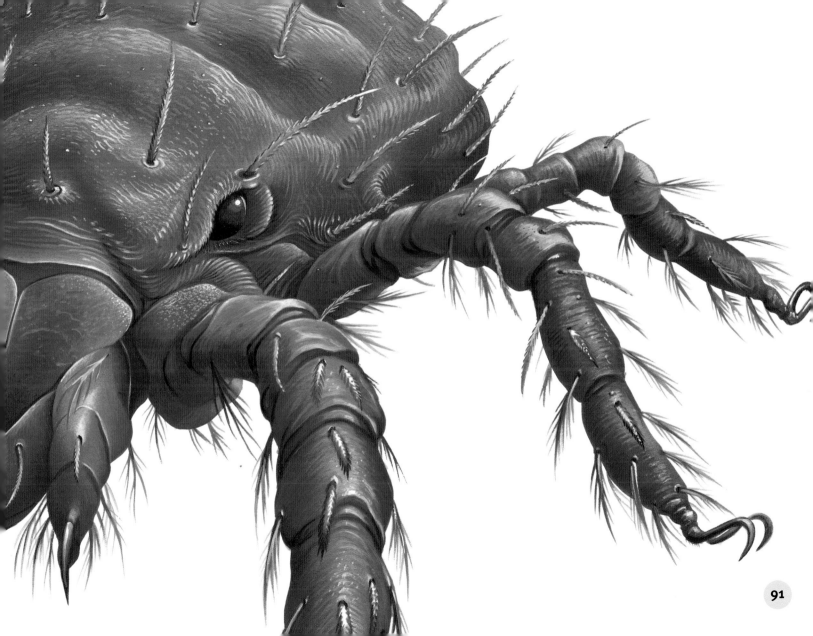

Fleas, Lice, Mites, and Ticks

Chigger Mite

These tiny creatures feed off other animals. They begin by eating dead skin, but eventually they reach the living layers, which is when their presence gets really irritating!

Dust Mite

These mites can be found wherever there is household dust. It's this mix of dirt, pollen, dead skin, and hair that dust mites find so irresistible.

Did you know?
Hard ticks eat just three times in their lives—twice when they change from juvenile to adult and once before they mate.

Hard Tick

These ticks start their lives among vegetation, where females lay their eggs. Once hatched, the larvae attach themselves to an animal host and feed on its blood.

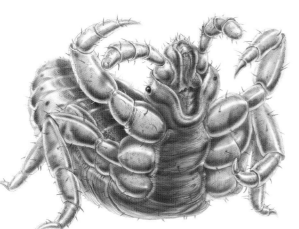

Human Louse

There are two types of these unpopular bugs—head and body. Body lice lay their eggs on clothing; head lice deposit their eggs (sometimes called "nits") in hair.

FACT-TASTIC

Plague fleas carry the bubonic plague (or "Black Death"). In the 14th century, this disease killed a quarter of the population of Europe.

Plague Flea

These tiny insects are one of the biggest killers in history. They suck the blood of their victims and so pass diseases from host to host.

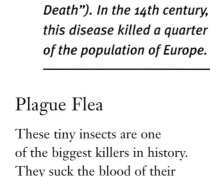

Chigger Flea

Chiggers are the smallest known species of flea. Rather than simply biting their hosts, newly mated females burrow into the soft skin beneath toenails, causing painful itching.

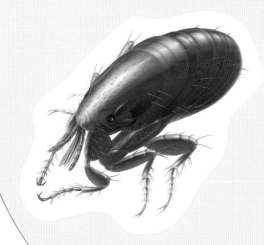

Tree stump

You might find stag beetles, termites, or earwigs crawling over a dead tree stump like this, and there could even be wasps and hornets nearby. Complete this scene with your animal stickers.

Wasps and Bees

One look at these boldly colored insects is enough to tell us that wasps and bees are closely related. What might be surprising, however, is just how many species of these furry-bodied insects there are. There are at least 17,000 species of wasps and 20,000 different types of bees! To keep things simple, though, most scientists divide them into "solitary" and "social" species. For example, cicada-killer wasps, which live alone in small nests or in underground burrows, are solitary. By contrast, honeybees, which live in complex nests and highly structured colonies, are social.

These amazing creatures are often called "the gardener's friends." That's because they play an important role in helping to pollinate plants. As adults, most wasps and bees feed on the nectar of flowers, which they gather by traveling from plant to plant. As they do this, they also pick up pollen and transfer it from male to female plants. This means that an active bee colony in your garden is helping plants to reproduce. Many species of wasps and bees also feed their young on insects such as weevils and cicadas, which are well-known plant pests. Consequently, these four-winged insects are very welcome guests in a garden!

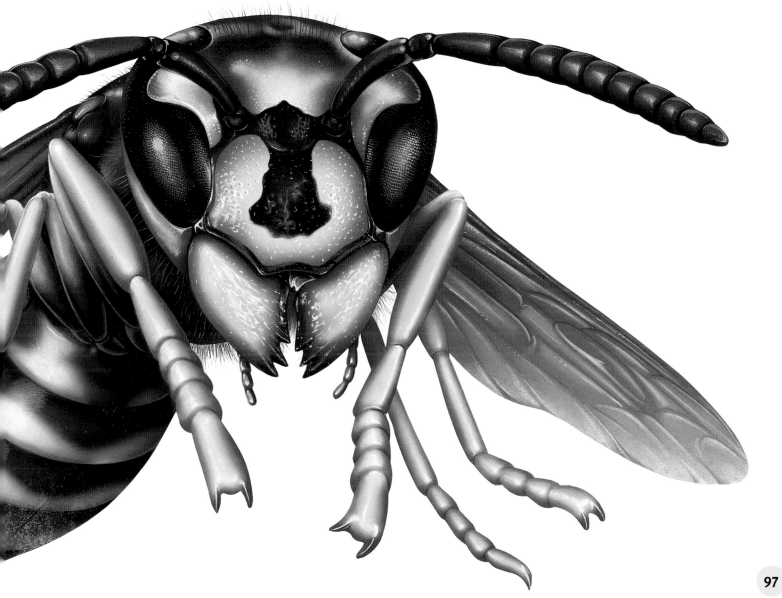

Wasps and Bees

Cicada-killer Wasp

Cicada-killer wasp burrows are usually built in dry, sandy soil, which means that they're often found in golf courses, driveways, and well-drained gardens in the eastern United States.

 FACT-TASTIC
The largest known species of bee is the giant honeybee. These massive insects grow to around eight inches long!

Common Wasp

Common wasps are social and widespread insects. Just like ants, they live together in large and complex colonies, which provide protection for the queen and her young.

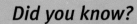
Did you know?
Over an entire lifetime, an average-sized honeybee collects enough nectar to make around one and a half ounces of honey.

Bee-killer Wasp

Bee-killers have a grisly start to life. Their eggs are laid in the bodies of captured honeybees. When they hatch, the growing larvae eat the living bee from the inside out.

Cuckoo Wasp

Like its bird namesake, female cuckoo wasps rely on others to raise their young by laying their eggs in the nests of other species of wasps.

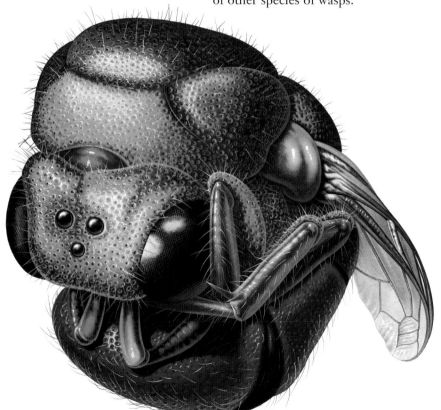

European Hornet

Hornet nests are made out of paper that the queen creates using chewed-up wood pulp. The nests are usually built in trees or the eaves of houses.

99

▶UP CLOSE: **European Hornet**

These large and beautifully patterned insects can be found throughout Europe and Asia, from southern England to Mongolia, although they are becoming increasingly rare in many regions.

The bold black and yellow stripes that can be seen on the bodies of most species of social wasps aren't just for decoration. They are a warning to predators to keep their distance.

Hornets, like all wasps, have four wings and six legs. When these large insects are at rest, these wings are usually folded beside the body, rather than across.

❗ FACT-TASTIC

If a hornet's nest overheats because of the number of insects buzzing around inside, workers gather at the entrance and fan their wings to ventilate it!

At the tip of the hornet's abdomen is its stinger, which is used to inject poison into prey. Hornets are highly sensitive and will readily sting anyone who disturbs them or their nest.

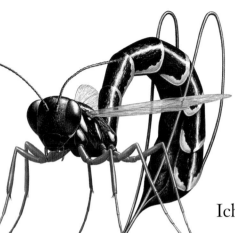

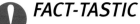
❗ FACT-TASTIC
Bees have been found trapped in amber (a type of fossilized tree sap) that dates back around 80 million years.

Ichneumon Wasp

The animal kingdom is a strange place. These slender-bodied insects feed their young on the larvae of other species, but as adults eat almost nothing but nectar.

Paper Wasp

Wasps were the world's first paper manufacturers! Using a combination of chewed wood mixed with saliva, paper wasp queens construct "papier-mâché" nests for their young.

Killer Bee

These famously aggressive bees are the result of selective breeding—mating European with African honeybees in an attempt to produce a species that makes more honey.

Wasps and Bees

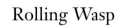

Rolling Wasp

Female rolling wasps usually have no wings. This means that the males (shown here) often have to carry them from flower to flower—attached tail to tail—while mating.

Tarantula Hawk Wasp

Female tarantulas are the prey of these skillful hunters. That's because they're bigger than the males and so provide more food for the wasp's quickly growing young.

Spider-hunting Wasp

These wasps paralyze spiders with powerful chemicals injected through the stinger. Then the spiders are dragged to the burrow to provide food for the wasp young.

▶UP CLOSE: **Tarantula Hawk Wasp**

As their name suggests, these wasps prey on tropical spiders—tarantulas. They are lone hunters: even males and females live and hunt separately and only come together to breed.

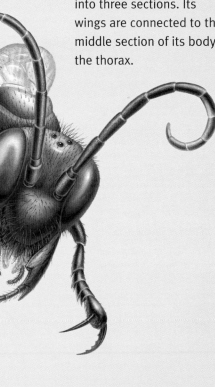

The biggest of the spider hunters, these cunning predators can grow up to three inches long, depending on which one of the 4,000 species they belong to.

A wasp's body is divided into three sections. Its wings are connected to the middle section of its body, the thorax.

Combats between wasps and tarantulas can be ferocious, but the wasps have a cunning technique. Once the spiders rear up to bite, they quickly insert their stingers.

Worms, Leeches, and Slugs

Not all animals walk or fly. Some of them slither and wriggle!

Worms, leeches, and slugs are perhaps the least complicated members of the animal kingdom. These soft-bodied creatures usually have no legs, eyes, or ears, and they often just have simple openings in their heads to take in food.

These uncomplicated animals don't have backbones or even a tough external skeleton to support their bodies, like crabs and most insects. So, even if they had legs it would be difficult for them to walk. Instead, to move they must expand and contract their muscular bodies. This creates a rippling movement that enables them to push through soil, vegetation, and water.

These unremarkable-looking creatures have a remarkable characteristic. They're usually hermaphrodites. This means that their bodies contain both male and female organs. This makes finding a mate somewhat easier. Some worms don't even need a mate at all, because they can reproduce by splitting themselves in two.

Worms, Leeches, and Slugs

Aquatic Leech

Once these soft-bodied worms have attached themselves to a host, they begin to feed—swelling to many times their size as their bodies fill with blood.

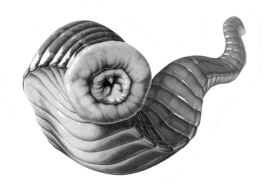

Fireworm

Fireworms are related to earthworms. However, unlike the useful garden variety, these water-living species are highly destructive, feeding on the tiny creatures that form coral reefs.

Did you know?
It's believed that bobbit worms may live for over a hundred years—and they continue to grow throughout their lives!

Bobbit Worm

Growing to seven feet long, these massive worms are true sea monsters. They make their homes in coral reefs, where they eat shrimp and fish.

Great Gray Slug

A slug has a unique way of moving around. It ripples its muscles, and the movement propels it along on one huge "foot," leaving a trail of slime behind.

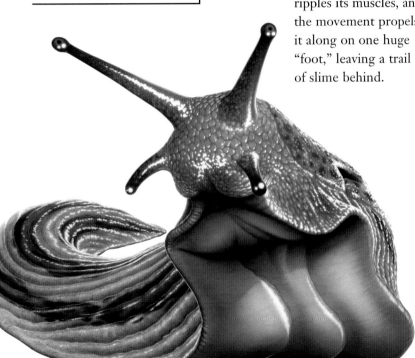

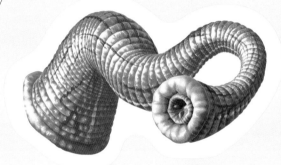

Land Leech

Land leeches are a type of worm whose bodies are divided into 34 segments. These well-known bloodsuckers can be found wherever there is water or damp vegetation.

Worms, Leeches, and Slugs

Tapeworm

Tapeworms don't need to hunt for food because they get all the nutrients they need by living inside the intestines of other animals—and that includes humans!

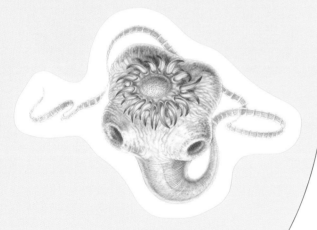

Velvet Worm

Velvet worms are able to overpower prey many times their own size by using a strong, gluey substance that they squirt from glands located in their heads.

▶UP CLOSE: **Tapeworm**

Horribly, millions of people worldwide are infected with tapeworms. These snakelike parasites develop inside the bodies of other animals. They are then passed on to humans when infected, undercooked meat is eaten.

Rows of spines help the tapeworm cling onto the wall of the gut. Once attached, the worm acts just like a part of the stomach, soaking up nutrients from the food that the host has eaten.

A tapeworm's body is made up of three parts: the head, the neck, and long, chainlike body segments. The worm "reproduces" by adding new body segments.

As the tapeworm grows, new body segments are added— about ten a day! These segments, which contain eggs, eventually drop off and leave the host's body with other waste products.

Other Creepy Crawlies

Of all the species that make their homes on our planet, over 70 percent are invertebrates—animals without backbones. Of these, the majority are insects and arthropods. An arthropod is an animal with a tough outer shell, jointed legs, and a body that is divided into segments.

At any one time, it's estimated that there are around ten quintillion (that's a ten followed by eighteen zeros) insects on our planet! Most of the time these tiny beasts go unnoticed, hidden away in the dirt, beneath floorboards, or camouflaged by vegetation. And often, when we do notice them, it's because they're pests that eat our food or carry dangerous diseases. Yet without them the world would be very different.

All animals have their place in the complex web of life. Within this web, every creature relies on every other. Silverfish, for example, can be a nuisance. They invade our homes and like to make a meal of everything from flour to wallpaper paste. But these flat, wingless insects provide food for a wide range of other animals, including spiders. If we were to take them away, then many of the animals that prey on them would vanish, too. So "creepy crawlies" like these are vital to the survival of many other species.

Other Creepy Crawlies

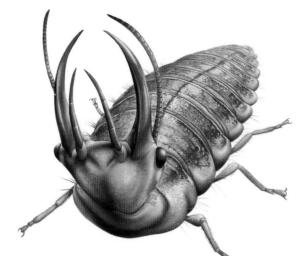

Common Lacewing

Most adult lacewings are gentle, pale-green vegetarians with four delicate wings. However, their larvae, as shown here, look quite different and are fearsome hunters.

Common European Earwig

The name "earwig" comes from the Old English *earwicga*, which means "ear beetle." The ancient Romans used to grind up these common insects to treat ear infections.

Ant Lion

Ant lion larvae, shown here, are remarkable engineers. These fat, hairy grubs dig deep, funnel-shaped pits. There they spend the next three years feeding on any insects that fall in!

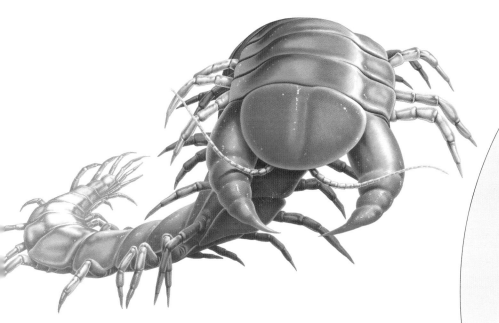

Giant Millipede

In Latin, *milli* means "thousand" and *pede* means "legs." Millipedes don't really have a thousand legs, just 100 to 400, depending on the species and their age.

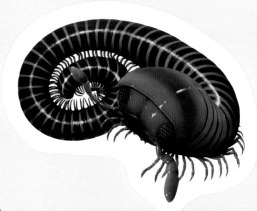

Giant Centipede

Despite their name, giant centipedes don't have a hundred legs, just a pair for each section of their bodies, usually between 30 and 46 in total.

▶UP CLOSE: Giant Millipede

Despite their name, none of these brightly colored creatures are really giants. They vary in size from around one-tenth of an inch to twelve inches in length.

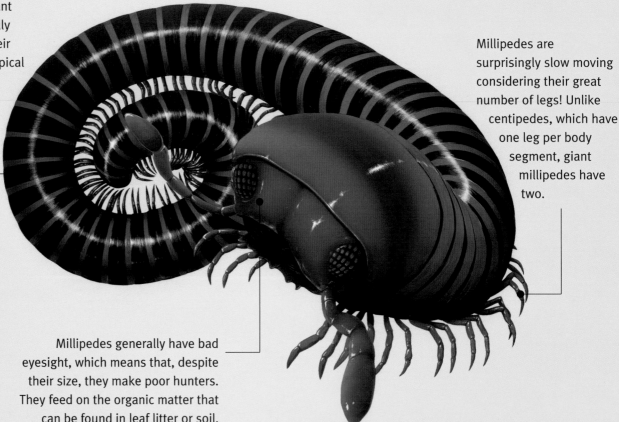

Many species of giant millipedes, especially those that make their homes in warm, tropical regions, are quite poisonous. Their bodies are brightly colored to warn predators away.

Millipedes are surprisingly slow moving considering their great number of legs! Unlike centipedes, which have one leg per body segment, giant millipedes have two.

Millipedes generally have bad eyesight, which means that, despite their size, they make poor hunters. They feed on the organic matter that can be found in leaf litter or soil.

Harvestman

The harvestman may look like a spider, but it's not. This curious creature gets its common name from its habit of gathering in large groups just before harvesttime.

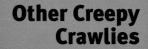

Did you know?
Dragonflies have compound eyes that contain more than 28,000 lenses. This gives them excellent eyesight for hunting insects and small tadpoles.

Hawker Dragonfly

In Europe, hawker dragonflies are sometimes called darners. This strange name refers to a folk tale that claims that they sew up children's lips during the night!

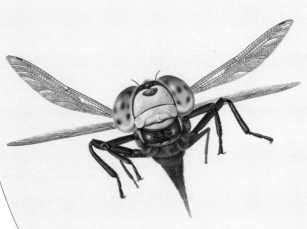

Leaf Insect

These remarkable creatures have developed to look just like the leaves and foliage that are most common in their rain-forest homes.

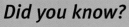

115

▶UP CLOSE: **Leaf Insect**

Leaf insects resemble leaves so closely that it has been known for other plant-eating insects to take bites out of them, mistaking them for a real juicy leaf!

 FACT-TASTIC

Leaf insects don't just imitate healthy leaves— many look like the brown and rotten ones found on a forest floor.

The abdomen is so flat and leaflike that it will catch the breeze and move gently, just like a real leaf. These creepy crawlies really are masters of disguise!

The leaf insect's jaws are quite small, but they are sharp enough to shred the leaves that it eats.

The legs look like leaves that have been almost completely eaten away. To get away from a predator, a leaf insect can lose one of its legs and still survive.

Silverfish

These primitive, wingless insects get their common name from the silvery scales that cover their flat bodies, combined with the swimming motion that they use to move.

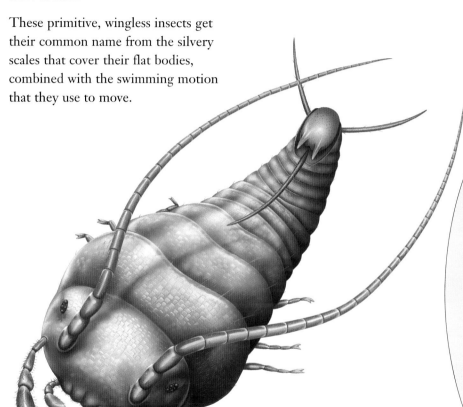

Common Scorpion Fly

Common scorpion flies are often mistaken for crane flies, which usually have clear wings. These slow-moving insects feed on nectar, fruit, or dead and dying insects.

Desert scrub

Out in the hot, dry desert, you might find snakes and scorpions, as well as lizards such as the Salvador's monitor, hunting for their next meal. Complete this desert scene with your animal stickers.

Lizards

It's easy to see lizards as nasty, scaly creatures. However, there's more to these tough-skinned reptiles than meets the eye.

Mammals—the group of creatures that includes humans—are warm-blooded. This means that their blood is heated inside the body by burning food for fuel. Reptiles, such as lizards, are cold-blooded. They can't control their own body temperatures; so, to stay alive, they have to avoid very hot or very cold weather. This is why lizards are often seen basking in the early morning sun to warm themselves up. In their unwarmed state, they're slow and sluggish, but once they've reached a comfortable temperature they're fast, agile, and skilled hunters.

These amazing reptiles have managed to make homes for themselves in some of the world's hottest deserts and wettest rain forests. There are species that live in the treetops, others that spend most of their lives in the water, and there are even some species that can fly. If the weather gets too hot, they find a shady spot for shelter. And if it gets cold, they simply go to sleep—hibernate—until the weather improves!

Lizards

Jackson's Chameleon

These famous lizards can alter their skin color. This happens in response to changes in the environment, rather than as a direct attempt to blend in with their surroundings.

FACT-TASTIC
Some lizards can shed their tails. This distracts predators long enough for the lizard to escape. The tail grows back later.

Ground Chameleon

Dressed in an array of spines and horny plates with a brown, earthy coloration, these tiny (one to four inches long) reptiles are virtually invisible in their natural habitat.

Did you know?
Autotomy is the ability of reptiles to regrow lost body parts. Occasionally, this goes wrong, resulting in two or more tails!

Green Iguana

Young iguanas have spectacular bright green and blue markings. These colors tend to become less dramatic with age, although many adults develop orange marks on their front legs.

Panther Chameleon

Lizards are some of nature's most colorful creatures. None more so than the spectacular panther chameleons, which come in an amazing selection of hues and tones.

Shingleback Skink

For the shingleback and many other Australian skinks, sticking out a vivid blue tongue is an extremely effective way of startling would-be attackers.

Leaf-tailed Gecko

Geckos are easy to identify because of their flattened bodies and the sticky pads on their hands and feet, which help them walk with ease on vertical surfaces.

Lizards

Chuckwalla

Despite their appearance, chuckwallas are shy creatures. If approached, they'll retreat to the nearest rock crevice and inflate their lungs, which makes them hard to remove by force.

Basilisk Lizard

Reaching speeds up to seven and a half miles per hour, basilisks can even run on water for brief periods. This ability has earned them the nickname "Jesus lizards."

Bearded Dragon

If threatened, an adult male dragon opens its mouth to inflate a collar of stiff spines (its "beard"). This lies in a circle around its blunt, triangular head.

▶UP CLOSE: **Basilisk Lizard**

Found mainly in Mexico and parts of Central America, these bright green vegetarians are just as comfortable in the water as they are among the treetops.

❗ FACT-TASTIC

In classical myths, a basilisk was a giant serpent that could kill its victims simply by looking at them.

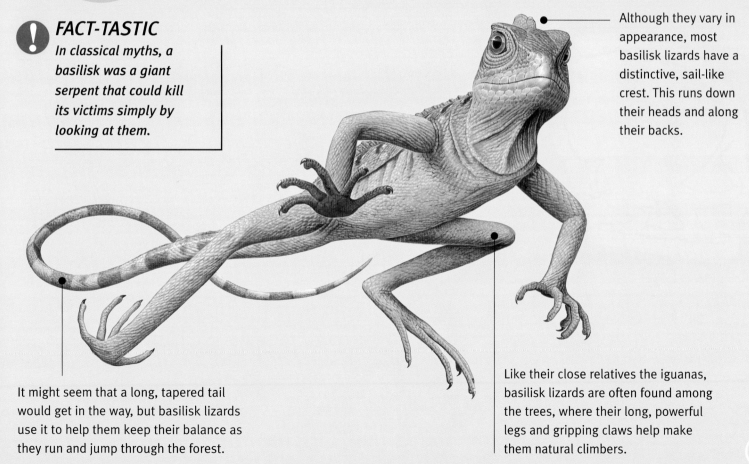

Although they vary in appearance, most basilisk lizards have a distinctive, sail-like crest. This runs down their heads and along their backs.

It might seem that a long, tapered tail would get in the way, but basilisk lizards use it to help them keep their balance as they run and jump through the forest.

Like their close relatives the iguanas, basilisk lizards are often found among the trees, where their long, powerful legs and gripping claws help make them natural climbers.

Lizards

Flying Lizard

Southeast Asia's lizards don't really fly, they glide, using elongated ribs that extend out from the body to support a thin membrane of skin, like a hang glider.

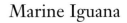

Did you know?
On average, a flying lizard can glide around 200 feet, controlling its flight by moving its wing membrane and tail.

Frilled Lizard

To scare predators away, frilled lizards flip open a large flap of skin around their necks, like an umbrella, creating frills up to eight inches in diameter.

Marine Iguana

Many lizards are perfectly at home in the water, but the unique marine iguana, found only on the Galápagos Islands, is the world's only truly aquatic lizard.

FACT-TASTIC

When under attack, a regal horned lizard can produce a strong jet of blood from its eyes!

Regal Horned Lizard

This spiny member of the iguana family is also known as a horned toad because of its flat, squat body, which resembles a toad's.

Nile Monitor

With their large, powerful legs, these big lizards are suited to life in a wide variety of habitats—they are good climbers, excellent burrowers, and skilled swimmers.

127

▶UP CLOSE: **Nile Monitor**

Although these big and bulky reptiles are a familiar sight on Egypt's Upper Nile River, Nile monitors also make their homes along Africa's coastal regions and in swamplands.

In common with all species of monitor lizards, the Nile variety has a long and powerful tail. This is often used in preference to teeth for defense.

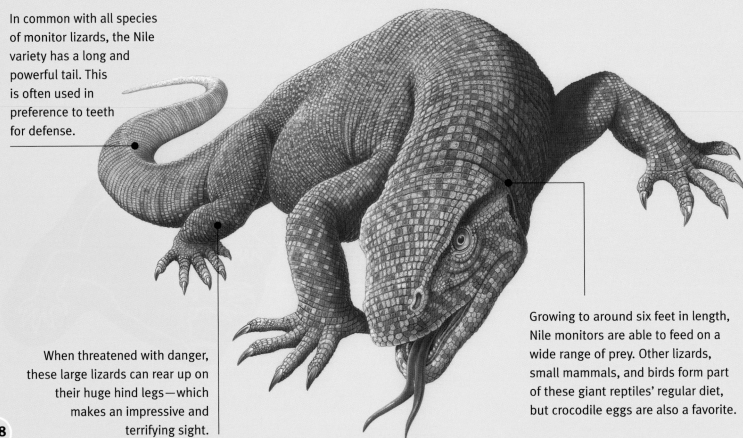

When threatened with danger, these large lizards can rear up on their huge hind legs—which makes an impressive and terrifying sight.

Growing to around six feet in length, Nile monitors are able to feed on a wide range of prey. Other lizards, small mammals, and birds form part of these giant reptiles' regular diet, but crocodile eggs are also a favorite.

Salvador's Monitor

These massive lizards are known in Papua New Guinea as "tree crocodiles" due to their scary habit of dropping down from trees to carry away domestic animals!

 FACT-TASTIC

Salvador's monitors are the longest lizards in the world. Two-thirds of their 18-foot length is made up of the tail.

Sandfish Skink

With their long bodies and tiny limbs, skinks may look like snakes, but they're lizards whose bodies have adapted to a life spent burrowing through the desert sand.

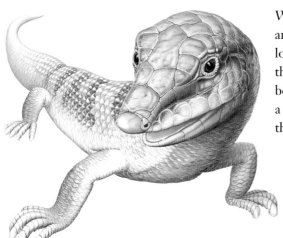

Savanna Monitor

During the wet season, these ravenous reptiles eat a tenth of their own body weight in food every day. These reserves are vital for survival in the dry season.

Lizards

Thorny Devil

This lizard's spiny body helps it survive in the desert. Each of its "thorns" is arranged so that rainwater is automatically channeled downward, toward its mouth.

Sun-gazer Lizard

A South African legend says that sun-gazers always face the sun. These lizards do seem to like nothing better than sunbathing at the entrance to their burrows.

Did you know?
Thorny devils are known by the scientific name Moloch horridus, *after the biblical demon Moloch.*

Tuatara

Tuatara aren't actually lizards, but the last survivors of a group of reptiles called sphenodonts. These are "living fossils" whose closest relatives died out 60 million years ago.

FACT-TASTIC

Green anoles can—and do—change color, but it's their vibrant green skin that tells us they're happy and healthy.

Lizards

Green Anole

American green anoles are quite a common sight on urban walls and fences, where their bright green bodies make these colorful reptiles extremely easy to spot.

Mexican Beaded Lizard

As one of the world's few poisonous lizards, these reptiles have a fearsome reputation. Their bite can be fatal to humans, although they usually only hunt rats.

Snakes

In myths and legends, they're seen as cunning, sly, and even evil, but snakes don't really deserve such a bad reputation.

There are around 2,700 species of snakes. These widespread reptiles vary in size from the tiny, tropical Brahminy blind snake, which grows to just six inches long, to the Asian reticulated python. These giant forest-dwellers can grow to 30 feet in length and can live for 70 years!

Like the python, all snakes are skilled hunters, using their forked tongues to taste the air and smell out a meal. They are fast and agile, using poison or the coils of their muscular bodies to kill their prey. They are also capable of killing and eating animals much larger than themselves. They do this by unhinging their jaws and swallowing their meals whole. Some pythons have even been known to eat leopards or bears! After such a huge meal, snakes can go many months without eating again. This means that they are remarkably adaptable. In fact, they can be found virtually all over the world. So, instead of calling them "cunning" and "sly," perhaps we should acknowledge the more positive qualities of these clever, wily—and deadly—creatures!

Snakes

King Cobra

King cobras are the world's largest venomous snake. Although their fangs are quite small, they can inject enough poison in just one bite to kill 20 people.

Did you know?
Anacondas are solitary, apart from during the breeding season, when up to 12 males form a "breeding ball" with the female.

! **FACT-TASTIC**
Snakes' jaws are not firmly attached to their skull, allowing them to open wide to swallow their prey.

Puff Adder

These stout snakes come in all shades of desert camouflage. They blend in so well with the environment that, lying completely still, they can become virtually invisible.

Anaconda

Anacondas spend most of their lives in or close to water. These huge constrictors are excellent swimmers and can hold their breath for up to ten minutes.

Bushmaster

In Latin, the South American Bushmaster's scientific name (*Lachesis muta*) means "silent fate." This evocative name is a tribute to this large and brightly patterned reptile's incredible hunting skills.

Brown Snake

Living in Australia can be hazardous to your health! Of the continent's estimated 120 poisonous snakes, its seven species of brown snakes are among the deadliest.

Golden Tree Snake

Taking off from the treetops, these snakes spread their ribs to create a stiff "parachute" that helps them to glide from tree to ground with ease.

135

Snakes

Asian Python

Pythons are constrictors.
Instead of using poison to kill, they
wrap their muscular bodies around
their victims, slowly tightening their
hold, until their prey suffocates.

Did you know?
*Some vipers' fangs are as long as
their heads. They fold back on
a hinged bone when they are
not in use.*

African Twig Snake

With long, slender
bodies, pointed heads,
and keyhole-shaped
pupils, twig snakes are
hard to mistake for
anything else. Which
is just as well, because
they're deadly!

Eyelash Viper

Found in central and northern
South America, these tree-dwellers
can be easily recognized by the
raised scales around their eyes that
give them their common name.

Death Adder

Australia is home to at least three species of these scarily named snakes. All are venomous and often use their thin tails as bait to attract prey.

Saw-scaled Viper

The name of these desert-dwelling snakes comes from the rows of slightly raised diagonal scales along the sides of their bodies that produce a sawlike sound.

❗ FACT-TASTIC
A rattlesnake's rattle, which contains eight segments, produces a warning sound that can be heard up to three feet away.

Western Diamondback Rattlesnake

Western diamondback rattlesnakes are highly poisonous, but their most famous feature, their rattle, is used for defense rather than offense, to warn intruders to keep well away.

Snakes

Asp Viper

A clue to the poisonous nature of these snakes is the two prominent bulges on either side of their wedge-shaped heads. These are their venom glands.

Rhinoceros-horned Viper

At rest, curled up in the undergrowth, these bulky snakes may seem sleepy, but during an attack they can propel themselves forward at ten feet per second.

Coral Snake

There are around 60 species of coral snakes. Their bands of red, black, and yellow make them one of the most visually striking types of snakes.

▶UP CLOSE: **Rhinoceros-horned Viper**

These brightly colored vipers of central and western Africa are easy to identify. In addition to their bold coloring, they have heavy, thickset bodies, short tails, and wide, almost triangular heads.

❗ FACT-TASTIC

If a rhinoceros-horned viper breaks a fang, it has up to six replacements growing at any one time—just in case!

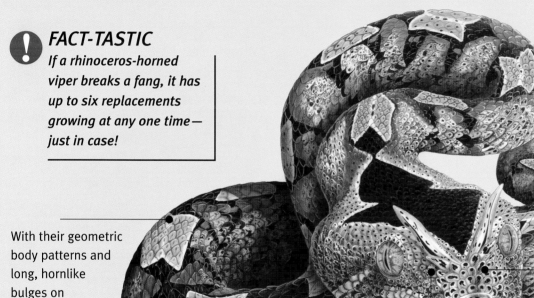

When snakes pull their tongues back into their mouths, microscopic scent particles are transferred to a specialized organ known as the Jacobson's organ.

With their geometric body patterns and long, hornlike bulges on their snouts, rhinoceros-horned vipers are one of the most curious and dramatic-looking members of the viper family.

The Jacobson's organ, combined with the snake's nostrils, provides an excellent sense of smell.

Snakes

Did you know?
It's believed that the ancestors of today's snakes evolved from lizards around 100 million years ago.

Fer-de-Lance

The fer-de-lance, or lancehead snake, got its unusual name from its V-shaped head. These look like the blunt lance tips once used by medieval knights.

Boomslang

In the Afrikaans language, the word *boom* means "tree" and *slang* means "snake." These long, slim, small-headed reptiles are South African tree snakes.

African Egg-eating Snake

Eating eggs three times the width of its own head is no problem for this snake! By unhinging their jaws, they're able to swallow the eggs quite easily.

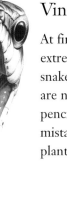

Vine Snake

At first glance, these extremely long, slender snakes (whose bodies are no thicker than a pencil) could easily be mistaken for a climbing plant or vine.

FACT-TASTIC

Black mambas are the sprinters of the snake world, capable of moving at speeds of about 11 miles per hour!

Black-necked Spitting Cobra

Spitting cobras' fangs curve upward. So, by flexing the muscles around their poison glands, they are able to spit their venom up to six feet.

Black Mamba

Surprisingly, black mambas aren't really black. As young juveniles, they're bright green. This color changes to a dark, gun-metal gray or muddy brown as they reach adulthood.

Snakes

Green Tree Python

At birth, green pythons are more likely to be red, yellow, brown, or orange than green. It's only as they mature that they begin to change color.

Tiger Snake

Typically, the bodies of these highly venomous snakes have 40 to 50 pale yellow or cream "tiger stripes," or waves, set against a green or brown background.

 FACT-TASTIC
Young tree pythons' tails have distinctive white markings that they use like bait to attract small prey.

Sea Krait

Broad scales under their bellies allow sea kraits to move easily on land, but they're equally at home in the sea, around coastlines from India to Australia.

▶UP CLOSE: **Sea Kraits**

Sea kraits may be perfectly at home in the ocean, but they are only temporary visitors. They still need to come back onto land during the winter breeding season in order to mate.

Unlike other species of snakes, sea kraits have flattened tails. This unusual shape, like a paddle, helps these brightly banded snakes propel themselves through the water.

The sea krait's body has been specially adapted for a life at sea. Its nostrils can be closed to keep out water when it dives below the waves in search of a meal of eels or fish.

Inside this very long body is a very long stomach! Snakes eat their prey whole, so this elongated stomach also needs to be very flexible.

143

Snakes

Asian Pit Viper

Like all pit vipers, Asian pit vipers (of which there are about 25 species) hunt using heat-sensitive pits just below their eyes, which help them to sense body heat.

Bush Viper

Like many tree-living species, bush vipers have long, gripping prehensile tails. These are used to hold on tightly to branches as they leap forward to catch prey.

Jumping Viper

These nocturnal (active at night) snakes have a very alarming habit. They throw themselves at their prey with such force that they leave the ground!

Did you know?
Snakes don't have eardrums, so they can't hear the music of snake charmers. It's the movement of the pipe that fascinates them.

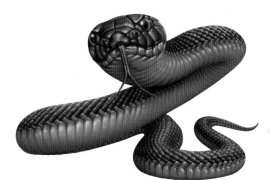

Red-bellied Black Snake

Numbers of this water-loving Australian species have fallen dramatically recently due to a plague of cane toads. These toads are eating a type of frog that is the snake's preferred food.

! FACT-TASTIC

Red-bellied black snakes can stay underwater for up to an hour before they need to come up for air.

Rainbow Boa

These large and spectacular South American forest-dwellers get their colorful common name from the brilliant, rainbowlike sheen that can be seen on their brightly colored scales.

Fierce Snake

This infamous reptile, also called a taipan, is the most toxic snake in the world. Just one bite from a fully grown adult is enough to kill 250,000 mice, its favorite food!

Snakes

Mangrove Snake

Most snakes will avoid trouble, but mangrove snakes are irritable and aggressive. They're poisonous, but they also use the coils of their bodies like constrictors to subdue their prey.

Asian Cobra

These snakes are also known as spectacled cobras due to the round marks on the back of their necks. In India they have a fearsome reputation as killers.

❗ FACT-TASTIC

Legends say that cobras got their "spectacles" when they used their hoods to shield the meditating Buddha from the midday sun.

Green Mamba

Mambas are highly poisonous. Luckily, in their natural forest homes, these slender snakes generally don't encounter many people. Most attacks occur when they're startled by plantation workers.

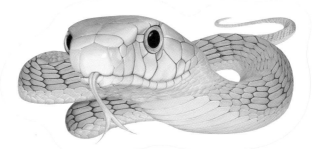

▶UP CLOSE: **Green Mamba**

Found in central and southern Africa, these deadly snakes are closely related to Asian cobras, although they lack the distinctive hood.

Green mambas are one of the few snakes to be uniformly green in color, although they're blue-green when young. This color provides them with excellent camouflage when hunting for small birds and reptiles among the forest foliage.

Many animals that live in the treetops have gripping, or prehensile, tails. This includes the green mamba, whose tapered tail is especially useful for hanging from trees when hunting.

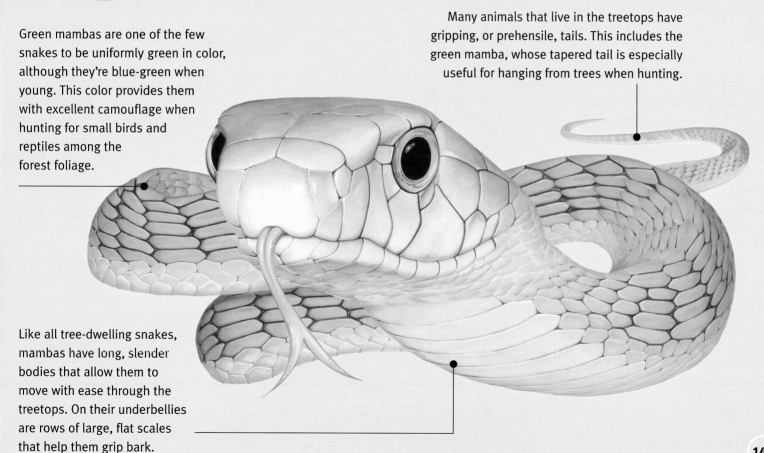

Like all tree-dwelling snakes, mambas have long, slender bodies that allow them to move with ease through the treetops. On their underbellies are rows of large, flat scales that help them grip bark.

Snakes

FACT-TASTIC

Snakes can be found everywhere except in the coldest regions and on isolated islands such as New Zealand and Ireland.

Cottonmouth Snake

Cottonmouth snakes get their rather strange name from the color of the inside of their mouths, which they show aggressively whenever they are in danger.

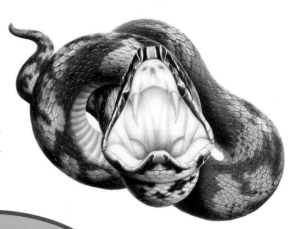

Did you know?
To avoid danger, snakes like ringhals and cobras play dead, rolling onto their backs and lying with their mouths open.

Long-nosed Tree Snake

Tree snakes can zero in on prey with incredible accuracy, using grooves that run from their eyes to the tips of their long snouts just like rifle sights.

Ringhals

The name *ringhals* (or *rinkhals*) comes from an Afrikaans word for "ringnecked." This refers to the pale bands that can be seen around the snake's neck and throat.

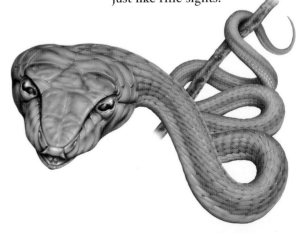

Massasauga

Like all rattlesnakes, Massasaugas use their rattles to warn predators to stay away. However, these dark-skinned snakes are so small, they produce more of a buzz than a full-blooded rattle.

Desert Horned Viper

Desert horned vipers hunt during the night. They bury themselves in the sand with just their heads showing and wait patiently for prey to pass by.

Gaboon Viper

These snakes need such large heads to hold their massive fangs! Gaboon vipers have the longest fangs of any snake, growing up to two inches in length.

Amphibians

Amphibians have an amazing claim to fame. They were probably the very first creatures with backbones to crawl out of the water and live on land. This wasn't something that happened overnight. It took place over many generations, as fish gradually developed lungs to breathe and learned how to use their fins to "walk."

However, these incredible creatures didn't completely leave their aquatic past behind them. Amphibians still need water to live. Most frogs, toads, and salamanders begin their lives as tiny eggs that are laid in ponds or streams, on vegetation, or among riverbed gravel. It's here that they are born, and it's where they spend their first few weeks before following the steps of their ancestors and moving onto land. As they do so, the fishlike tadpoles undergo an incredible change. They lose their gills and tails and begin to grow powerful legs and air-breathing lungs.

For around 100 million years, taking the giant step from water to land made amphibians the undisputed rulers of the earth. Today there are, sadly, far fewer of these fascinating creatures around, but their transformation from tadpoles into fully formed adults is just as remarkable.

Amphibians

Giant Salamander

Salamanders might look like lizards, but they're really slender, long-tailed amphibians. The champions of this group are Chinese giant salamanders, which can grow to 20 feet in length.

African Bullfrog

African bullfrogs are notoriously big eaters and will attempt to make a meal of practically anything that they can cram into their mouths, even poisonous snakes!

Axolotl

Most young amphibians live in water. Over time, they grow lungs and legs and move onto land. Axolotls are unusual because they remain in their larval form for their entire lives.

▶UP CLOSE: **African Bullfrog**

Most amphibians spend their lives in or close to fresh water, but African bullfrogs live on Africa's dry grasslands. These remarkable frogs live in underground burrows, coming out in the cool evenings to hunt.

Bullfrogs don't need webbed feet to push them through the water. Instead, they have powerful, unwebbed front legs that help them hold on to and subdue prey.

During the dry season, these bullfrogs dig down into the soil, where they form cocoons of shed skin and mucus around themselves. There they wait patiently for the rains to come.

Three sharp teeth, which are hidden away in the frog's bottom jaw, are used to help these broad-bodied amphibians keep a tight grip on struggling prey.

Amphibians

Malaysian Horned Toad

Horned toads aren't especially active. They take a patient approach to hunting, using their camouflage to lie hidden under leaves on the forest floor until prey passes by.

FACT-TASTIC
Amphibians swallow their food whole. The size of a meal is only limited by the size of their mouths.

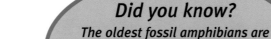

Did you know?
The oldest fossil amphibians are 360 million years old. They were probably the first vertebrates to leave the water for land.

Budgett's Frog

When eating, these powerful amphibians use their unwebbed forearms to cram food into their mouths, using two toothlike projections in their lower jaws to hold their prey secure.

Fire-bellied Toad

This toad's bright colors are used to warn away predators. Should this fail, it also produces a foul-tasting mucus that persuades most hunters to spit it out!

Mantella Frog

These little frogs hunt by day, with little fear of attack from predators. The reason for this apparent lack of concern is simple. They are highly toxic!

Cane Toad

Cane toads are also known as marine toads, although they don't live in oceans. They prefer the slightly salty waters where river estuaries meet the sea.

Ornate Horned Frog

Ornate frogs are found in South America's dense, lush rain forests. These plump amphibians make their homes in damp burrows beneath thick leaf litter on the forest floor.

Amphibians

Paradoxical Frog

Paradoxical frogs spend more of their lives as tadpoles than do other species of frogs. This valuable extra time allows them to grow up to a remarkable ten inches in length.

Poison-dart Frog

Dart frogs use small pools of water that collect in the hollows of leaves as nurseries for their tadpoles. Here they're fed by their parents until they are mature.

Suriname Toad

This toad has one of the more unusual breeding habits of any animal. Once the eggs are fertlized, the male presses them into the female's back, where skin grows over the eggs. A few months later, the young froglets emerge from the mother's back!

▶UP CLOSE: **Paradoxical Frog**

A paradox is something that goes against common sense, but is still true. The paradoxical frog lives up to its name—the adults are a fourth the size of the tadpoles.

FACT-TASTIC
Scientists are still not sure why the paradoxical frog shrinks as it gets older.

This paradoxical frog—also known as the shrinking frog—is shown here partway through the process of changing from a tadpole to an adult. It has grown its legs but still has a tail.

Like other frogs, as they metamorphose into adults, tadpoles lose their tails and exchange their gills (which allow them to breathe underwater) for lungs.

In order to get enough fuel for their amazing change from tadpole into adult, the tadpoles feed on the algae in the water. As adults, they eat mainly insects.

Tropical sea

The tropical seas and oceans are home to many amazing creatures, from stonefish to sea horses, as well as octopus, squid, and crabs. Complete this underwater scene with your animal stickers.

Crustaceans and Mollusks

It's estimated that there are around 42,000 species of crustaceans worldwide. Members of this animal group usually live in the ocean and include crabs, lobsters, crayfish, and shrimp. Like mollusks, crustaceans don't have any bones. Their soft bodies are instead protected by a stiff, tough outer shell. These shells act like an external skeleton. As crustaceans grow, they shed their shells and grow new ones that fit them better!

Most mollusks also make their homes in the oceans. This group of creatures represents the biggest order of water-living animals and includes an amazing array of weird and wonderful creatures—from eight-armed octopuses to snails that creep around on the ocean floor. Like crustaceans, mollusks have hard shells to protect their bodies. For clams, mussels, oysters, and whelks, however, these shells are their homes as well as their protection! Cuttlefish, squid, and octopuses are mollusks, too. So why don't they have shells? In fact, most of these species do have something similar to a shell, but they aren't immediately obvious because they grow inside their bodies!

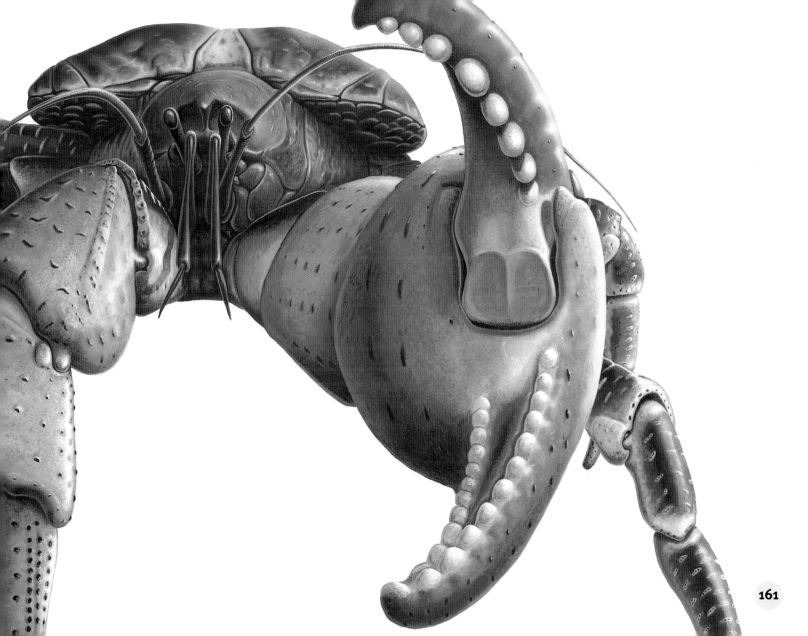

Crustaceans and Mollusks

Mantis Shrimp

Mantis shrimp are also known as "thumb choppers"! This is because they will lunge at any potential meal that comes their way using their huge, barbed claws.

Cone Shell

Found mainly in shallow waters, cone shells are patient predators who will often bury themselves in the mud, where they lie in wait for passing meals.

Did you know?
Dog whelks are able to follow prey over great distances. They hunt by tasting the water for their prey's chemical "scent."

Dog Whelk

The dog whelk is one of the ocean's many species of sea snails. Like its land-bound counterparts, it creeps across the seabed on one large, muscular foot.

Pistol Shrimp

Pistol shrimp have one huge claw. They use this to make shock waves in the water, bringing their pincers together with a loud snap. The vibrations stun their prey.

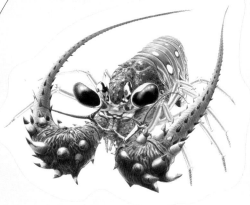

! FACT-TASTIC

Spiny lobsters have ten legs. These extra limbs enable these prickly crustaceans to run at up to 17 miles per hour.

Slipper Lobster

Slipper lobsters don't have pincers. Instead they use their large, flattened antennae to dig through the mud and sand of the seabed in search of food.

Spiny Lobster

All crustaceans have a thick external skeleton for protection, but spiny lobsters have gone one step further. Their tough outer shells are lined with thornlike spines.

163

Crustaceans and Mollusks

Harlequin Shrimp

Harlequin shrimp are shy creatures that only come out of their burrows at night to hunt. These small reef-dwellers mate for life and usually hunt in pairs.

Sea Slug

These soft-bodied mollusks, which are shell-less snails, are incredibly brightly colored. They often sport stripes or spots, with particularly bright colors on the hornlike lumps on their backs.

Cuttlefish

Cuttlefish are closely related to squid and octopus. Like their aquatic cousins, these creatures are considered to be more intelligent than other marine animals.

▶UP CLOSE: Harlequin Shrimp

It's the bold patterns on the bodies of harlequin shrimp that give them their unusual name. In the Middle Ages, harlequins were a type of clown, famous for their multicolored clothing.

Most shrimp have two pairs of feelers on their heads. These are used to help shrimp "taste" the water for chemical changes that tell them food is nearby.

A tough outer shell, called an exoskeleton, protects the shrimp's body. Because this shell is unable to grow with the shrimp like skin, the shrimp must shed, or molt, its shell regularly and grow a larger replacement.

Shrimps' bodies are divided into two parts: the cephalothorax (the combined head and chest) and the abdomen (the rear part of the body).

❗ FACT-TASTIC

Harlequin shrimp eat starfish, working from leg to leg. They even feed the starfish to keep them alive and fresh.

Nautilus

Nautiluses are cephalopods—a group that includes squids and octopuses. These primitive creatures have remained virtually unchanged for 500 million years, when their ancestors dominated the oceans.

Blue-ringed Octopus

When it is alarmed, a blue-ringed octopus's skin changes color to flash blue warning rings. The greater the danger, the brighter and faster the flashes.

Opalescent Squid

It's only in dark oceans that we see how this creature got its name. These intelligent beasts communicate using light-producing cells in their bodies to send messages. *Opalescent* means "reflecting iridescent (rainbow-colored) light."

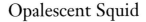

▶UP CLOSE: **Blue-ringed Octopus**

Despite its attractive color, the blue-ringed octopus is one of the world's most deadly species. A single bite is capable of killing a human in minutes.

❗ FACT-TASTIC
Octopus blood is different from that of mammals. For one thing, it is a shade of blue, rather than red.

Octopuses are very intelligent creatures. However, about two-thirds of their brain's "gray matter" is actually in their arms.

The bite of a blue-ringed octopus is painless, but it can cause paralysis. The victim's lungs and heart eventually stop working, and without treatment the victim will die.

A blue-ringed octopus female will lay only one clutch of about 50 eggs in her lifetime. These are incubated under her arms for six months.

Hermit Crab

Hermit crabs don't have shells of their own. Instead, they make their homes in discarded shells, especially those of whelks, which give them the protection they need.

Christmas Island Red Crab

There are so many of these large, bright red crabs on Christmas Island that they create total chaos during their annual migration to the seashore to breed.

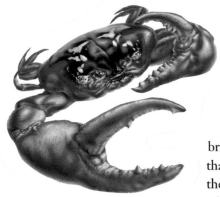

Did you know?

Migrating Christmas Island crabs follow routes their ancestors used before humans arrived on the island, regardless of what's in the way!

 FACT-TASTIC

If it finds a suitable shell with a hermit crab already living in it, a larger hermit crab will evict the occupant and move in!

Arrow Crab

Arrow crabs get their common name from their barbed beaks, which they use to spear and hold prey while their sharp pincers quickly tear apart the victim's flesh.

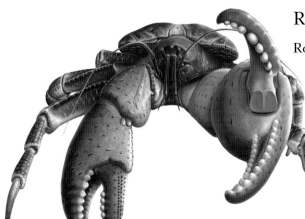

Robber Crab

Robber crabs are the world's largest land crabs. These huge crustaceans spend their entire adult lives on land, although females must lay their eggs in the sea.

Spider Crab

Japanese spider crabs, which can be found in the ocean depths off Japan, are the true giants of this species, with a recorded leg span of six and a half feet.

Horseshoe Crab

These unique creatures are the sole survivors of a group that has changed little since its ancestors roamed the oceans 300 million years ago in the Paleozoic era.

169

Other Sea Creatures

If you want to see real-life monsters, then you need look no further than in the oceans! Water covers the majority of our planet's surface, and most of it (around 70 percent) can be found in the five great oceans: the Pacific, the Atlantic, the Indian, the Arctic, and the Antarctic. It's believed that all life on earth began in these huge bodies of water, and an incredible variety of marine animals still make their homes in their depths.

Here, among seaweed forests, sunken mountain ranges, and coral reefs, it's possible to find an amazing array of creatures, many of which wouldn't look out of place on the set of a science-fiction movie! Take, for example, the gulper eel. These fantastic fish live in the deepest and darkest parts of the ocean. In this world, where the sun never shines, food is scarce, so the gulper eel's body has developed into a huge mobile sack with a vast mouth that trawls through the waters for food! Then there's the even odder deep-sea hatchetfish, whose axe-shaped body gives off an eerie blue light. Or the disgusting, slime-covered hagfish, which feeds on rotting flesh at the bottom of the ocean!

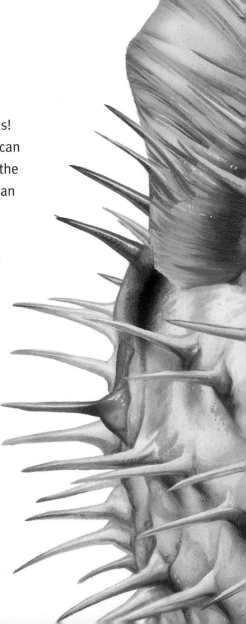

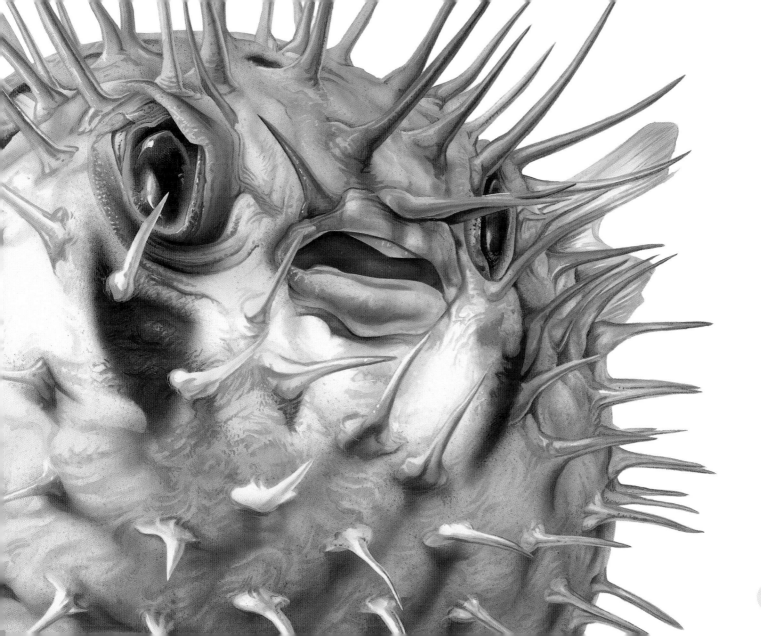

Other Sea Creatures

African Lungfish

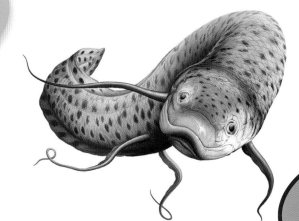

Lungfish have lungs, not gills, so these fish would drown if they didn't surface regularly to gulp air. This means they can live only in shallow water.

! *FACT-TASTIC*
Archerfish are able to leap up to a foot out of the water to snatch flying insects from the air.

Did you know?
African lungfish can hibernate for up to three years in clay balls on dried-up riverbeds. They breathe through tubes made of mucus!

Archerfish

These small, attractive fish have their own air-propelled missile system! They are able to shoot jets of water from their mouths, knocking land-bound prey into the water.

Alligator Gar

Like all fish, alligator gars have gills, but their swim bladders act like primitive lungs, allowing them to breathe air when a river's water level falls.

Box Jellyfish

The deadly box jellyfish has a square shape, with around 15 tentacles on each corner. Each of these tentacles is armed with about 500,000 toxic stinging cells.

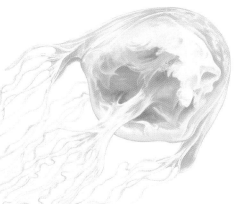

Crown-of-Thorns

Most starfish have five arms, but the crown-of-thorns starfish can have up to 23! These are covered with sharp, protective spines and are loaded with poisonous venom.

❗ FACT-TASTIC

Around 70 percent of all humans who are stung by box jellyfish die, often within just a few minutes.

Coelacanth

Until 1938, coelacanths were believed to be long extinct. Then one was caught at the mouth of the Chalumna River, off the eastern coast of South Africa.

Other Sea Creatures

Deep-sea Hatchetfish

Hatchetfish can't afford to waste energy. Food in the deep sea is scarce, so their bodies are a basic design: small, with compact fins and a huge mouth.

Deep-sea Gulper Eel

There's little to eat in the deep sea, so the gulper's body is little more than a mobile stomach, with a huge mouth at one end to sift for food.

! FACT-TASTIC
Electric eels can generate a powerful shock. These have been measured at up to 550 volts for a six-foot-long eel.

Electric Eel

In the slow-moving waters of the Amazon and Orinoco rivers lurks one of nature's most remarkable fish. Electric eels can generate short bursts of electricity to stun prey.

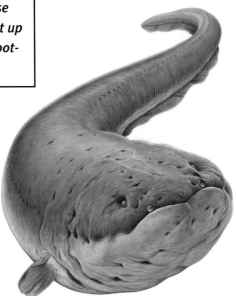

▶UP CLOSE: **Deep-sea Gulper Eel**

The reason these fish look so bizarre is because their bodies have adapted to live in one of the world's most extreme environments—up to 10,000 feet down in the gloomy ocean depths.

The gulper eel's body has been pared down to the bare essentials to save energy. Its scaleless body is narrow, with small fins and a slender tail.

At the other end of this amazing body is a thin tail tipped with a glowing "lure" that is used to attract prey or a mate.

A gaping mouth continually sifts the waters for food such as small fish, crustaceans, and plankton. This mouth makes up two-thirds of the gulper eel's body and is generally lined with numerous pin-sharp teeth.

175

Other Sea Creatures

Electric Ray

Electric rays are shocking creatures! These flat-bodied fish are able to generate short bursts of electric current—up to 200 volts—which they use to stun prey.

European Conger Eel

These powerful eels are surprisingly shy and, when they are seen, divers will often spot just a large, powerful head jutting out from a hiding spot.

Did you know?
A starfish has no central brain—just a ring of nerves and long nerve fibers running up each arm, which allow it to react to movement and light.

European Starfish

Each of this creature's five arms contains reproductive organs. So, even if three of its arms are eaten, it can still regrow most of its lost body!

Frogfish

These strange-looking fish are similar in appearance to the coral reefs among which they live. This makes it difficult for predators and divers to find them.

Anglerfish

Anglerfish are also known as goosefish and monkfish. On a spine between its eyes is a flexible "rod" tipped with a lure, which it uses to "fish" for food.

Hagfish

This pale, wormlike creature has no eyes, no stomach, and no jaw. Its main weapon is a long, rasping tongue that is covered with toothlike projections.

❗ FACT-TASTIC
It only takes about a hundredth of a second for a frogfish to open its mouth and suck in its prey!

177

▶UP CLOSE: **Anglerfish**

Anglerfish get their common name from the way they catch their prey, "fishing" with a flexible rod attached between their eyes.

The tails of some species of anglerfish, known as monkfish, are a popular food and appear daily at seafood stores around the world. The heads are often not displayed, as they scare customers!

The 300 species of anglerfish found around the world can be identified by their flat bodies as well as their gaping mouths.

When prey attempts to take the fake bait, the anglerfish simply opens its mouth and sucks in its prey whole.

! *FACT-TASTIC*
Most species of anglerfish live in the deep oceans where the sun's light cannot penetrate. Their lures glow in the dark.

Leafy Sea Dragon

Australia's leafy sea dragons are close relatives of sea horses, although they're slightly larger in size, with "leaf sprout" camouflage covering their bodies.

Lionfish

Their bold coloring has earned lionfish the names turkeyfish, dragonfish, and firefish. When young, they're almost transparent, but as adults they have distinctive stripes and featherlike fins.

Lion's Mane Jellyfish

These amazing-looking creatures are the world's largest species of jellyfish. Their thick, bell-shaped bodies can reach up to a foot across, with toxic tentacles growing to six and a half feet long.

Other Sea Creatures

North American Sea Nettle

Sea nettles are a serious hazard to swimmers. These bell-shaped jellyfish are unusual in that they prefer river estuaries to the salty waters of the open ocean.

Mudskipper

These odd fish spend more time out of the water than in it! Using fins and their powerful tails, they're even able to "walk" on land with slow, jerky motions.

 FACT-TASTIC

Oarfish may have been the inspiration behind many of the myths told about sea serpents, including the Loch Ness Monster.

Oarfish

Little is known about these secretive giants of the sea, which are believed to be the largest bony fish in the world, because few have ever seen an oarfish alive.

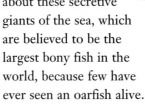

▶UP CLOSE: **Mudskipper**

These amphibian-like fish are a common sight on mudflats and in swamps throughout Africa, Asia, and Australia. They can often be seen crawling from their underground burrows at low tide to feed.

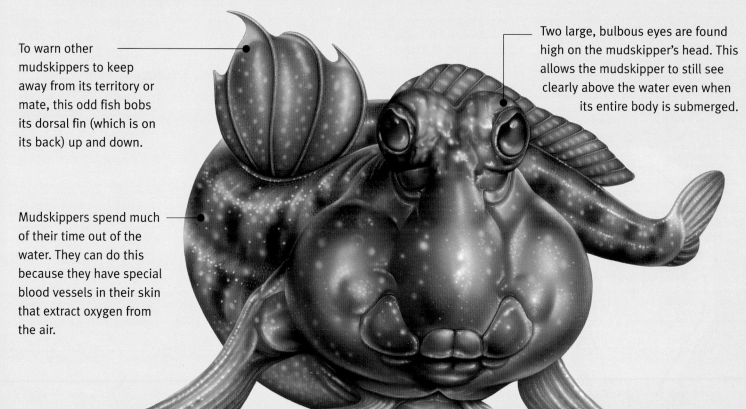

To warn other mudskippers to keep away from its territory or mate, this odd fish bobs its dorsal fin (which is on its back) up and down.

Mudskippers spend much of their time out of the water. They can do this because they have special blood vessels in their skin that extract oxygen from the air.

Two large, bulbous eyes are found high on the mudskipper's head. This allows the mudskipper to still see clearly above the water even when its entire body is submerged.

Other Sea Creatures

Piranha

When piranhas close their overlapping jaws, their flat, sharp, wedge-shaped teeth come together with such force that they slice circular hunks of flesh off their prey.

Ocean Sunfish

These disk-shaped fish are taller than they are wide, with skin so rough that it can take the paintwork off a ship's bow just by swimming past.

> **! FACT-TASTIC**
> A shoal of piranhas is capable of reducing a fully grown, 100-pound pig to bone in under a minute.

> **Did you know?**
> The sawfish's awesome weaponry is mainly used to dig for crustaceans and mollusks, which make up most of its diet.

Porcupine Fish

Just like puffer fish, porcupine fish can inflate their bodies to scare away predators. They do this by gulping down water until their stomachs are stretched and enlarged.

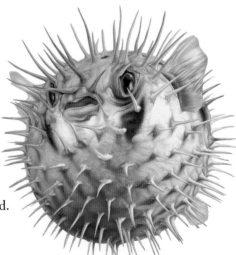

Portuguese Man-of-War

It used to be believed that these poisonous drifting masses were jellyfish. However, the truth is much stranger! A man-of-war is not one creature but rather a colony of separate, interdependent animals.

Sawfish

About a third of this fish's entire body length is made up of its characteristic "saw"—an elongated snout, studded with up to 30 peglike teeth.

Scorpion Fish

When hunting, scorpion fish open their mouths so quickly that they create a vacuum that can suck in prey half their total body size in less than a second.

▶UP CLOSE: Portuguese Man-of-War

Wherever the wind blows, this amazing colony of creatures follows. Portuguese man-of-wars were named after a type of ship, and like a ship, they are carried across the oceans by the wind.

! *FACT-TASTIC*

The Portuguese Man-of-War's "sail" is mainly filled with air, although sometimes it can contain deadly carbon monoxide.

The floating, multicolored canopy above the waves (called the pneumatophore) is the original colony "founder."

Poisonous stingers are so deadly that they kill prey in seconds. Once dead, the tentacles take the prey to the gastrozooids, which are the colony's feeding and reproductive organs.

Hanging below the canopy are dozens of deadly tentacles called dactylozooids. When prey is in sight, cells within these tentacles shoot out barbed stingers that embed themselves in the flesh.

Sea Anemone

Although they spend much of their time fixed to rocks, anemones can walk and even swim by moving their tentacles backward and forward and flexing their cylinder-shaped bodies.

Sea Horse

As they're toothless, sea horses feed mainly on small shrimp and plankton, which they are able to swallow whole, sucking them up through their long, tubular snouts.

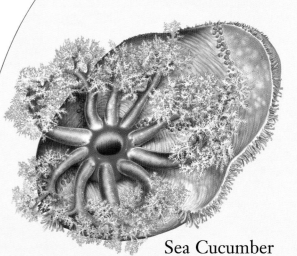

Sea Cucumber

Sea cucumbers have an incredible—and very useful—ability. When in danger, they can "liquefy" their bodies so that they can hide in the smallest of rock crevices.

Sea Lamprey

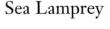

Inside the lamprey's mouth is a disk of spiny teeth and a rasping tongue that strips away scales and purees flesh, allowing it to suck down a liquid meal.

Did you know?
Sea robins are famous for the loud noises they make when they're distressed. These noises sound like a drum being beaten.

Sea Robin

Not all fish swim. Some, like sea robins, prefer to walk! These bizarre bottom-dwellers use their two pectoral fins like legs to crawl along the seabed.

Sea Urchin

The sea urchin's mouth is a unique apparatus—a series of five movable teeth that are so powerful they can gouge hiding places in rock.

Spotted Eagle Ray

Eagle rays are one of the most attractive species of rays. These graceful fish are powerful swimmers who use their fins like wings to glide through the ocean.

Stonefish

Lying still on the seabed, these lumpy, gray-brown fish are easily mistaken for a piece of rock. Many species even have algae growing on their skin!

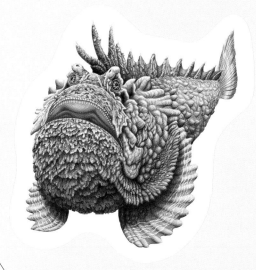

Stargazer

Stargazers are a bottom-dwelling species that spend much of their time buried in the soft mud of the seabed, lying in wait for prey.

 FACT-TASTIC
Stonefish are one of the ocean's most toxic fish. A sting is capable of killing a fully grown human.

Toadfish

These shy fish spend much of their time hiding in rock crevices or in specially dug holes. During the breeding season, these holes are turned into nests.

Did you know?
Toadfish are famous singers! In the early summer mating season, enthusiastic males will attempt to attract females by serenading them.

Tigerfish

Tigerfish are the African equivalent of South America's piranhas. Although these aggressive fish belong to different families, both have a fearsome reputation.

! FACT-TASTIC
Triggerfish are named after their stiff dorsal spikes. They can lock upright to prevent a predator from swallowing the fish whole.

Triggerfish

Triggerfish can be found around the coastlines of the world's warmer oceans. Their flattened bodies, long snouts, and small, tooth-lined mouths make them easy to identify.

Weaverfish

Unlike most fish, which have a gas-filled sac known as a swim bladder to help them stay afloat, weavers spend their time on the ocean floor, so they don't need one.

Wolffish

The wolffish's preferred food is crustaceans and mollusks. It usually eats these whole—shells and all! Its large teeth help break its food into manageable chunks.

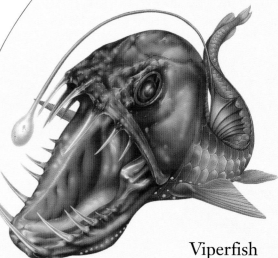

Viperfish

Viperfish are a fearsome sight. Yet there are few people who have seen this aggressive predator up close, as it lives from 600 to 3,000 feet down in the ocean's depths.

Glossary

Abdomen: Rear part of the body of an arachnid, bug, or insect.

Amphibian: A cold-blooded animal that usually hatches from an egg laid in water and develops into an adult that lives on land and looks very different from the young.

Antennae: Long, movable feelers on the heads of crustaceans, bugs, and insects, used mainly to find food.

Aquatic: Living in water.

Arachnid: An eight-legged arthropod with no antennae or wings.

Arboreal: Living in the trees.

Arthropod: An animal with a segmented body, jointed limbs, and a hard outer shell.

Beetle: An insect whose front wings have developed into hard, protective wing cases.

Bug: An insect with no chewing or biting mouthparts; instead, it sucks its food through a strawlike snout.

Camouflage: Color or body shape that allows an animal to blend in with its surroundings.

Carnivore: An animal that eats meat.

Cephalopod: An oceanic animal that usually has a large head and tentacles, such as a squid.

Cephalothorax: Combined head and middle body parts (thorax) of an arachnid.

Cocoon: Protective covering.

Cold-blooded: Animals whose body temperature depends on the temperature of their environment.

Colony: A group of animals that live together.

Compound eyes: Eyes that are made up of thousands of six-sided lenses, each of which shows part of the total image.

Constrictor: A snake that kills prey by suffocation.

Crustacean: An animal with a tough outer shell covering its body and, usually, jaws and gills. Most live in water.

Gills: Special organs on aquatic animals that allow them to breathe underwater.

Grub: *See* larvae.

Habitat: Natural home of an animal.

Herbivore: An animal that eats plants.

Insect: An invertebrate with a body divided into three sections, with three pairs of legs and one or two pairs of wings.

Invertebrate: An animal without a backbone.

Juvenile: A young animal.

Larvae: A stage in the change of an insect from an egg to an adult. Larvae may take the form of a grub, caterpillar, or maggot.

Lizard: A reptile that usually has an elongated body, four legs, and a long tail.

Maggot: The larval form of certain insects, such as flies.

Mammal: A warm-blooded, air-breathing animal that gives birth to live young.

Mandibles: Insect mouthparts, often forming powerful jaws.

Metamorphosis: The transformation of an insect from an egg to a larva, a pupa, and then an adult. Larvae may take the form of a grub, caterpillar, or maggot. Other insects have an incomplete metamorphosis, from egg to nymph.

Mollusk: An invertebrate with a soft, unsegmented body inside a tough shell.

Myriapod: Ground-dwelling creatures with long, segmented bodies and many legs, such as centipedes.

Nectar: Sugary liquid produced by plants and collected as food by many insects.

Nocturnal: Active during the night.

Nymph: Larvae of insects such as dragonflies or butterflies. Nymphs usually look like adults without wings.

Parasite: An animal that lives off (or in) the body of another animal, which is usually harmful to the "host" animal.

Predator: An animal that hunts others and eats their meat.

Prehensile: Adapted for grasping objects; many animals have hands or tails that are used in this way.

Pupa: An intermediate stage in the metamorphosis from larva to adult. Pupae don't feed and are often enclosed in a cocoon.

Reptile: A cold-blooded, air-breathing animal. Reptiles usually have scaly skin and lay eggs.

Spider: An eight-legged, silk-producing arachnid.

Swim bladder: An air-filled sac that helps animals stay afloat in water.

Tadpole: Larvae of frogs or toads.

Tarantula: Name given to large, hairy, tropical spiders.

Tentacle: An elongated "arm" used for grasping and feeding.

Thorax: The middle body segment of an insect.

Vertebrate: An animal with a backbone.

Warm-blooded: An animal whose body temperature is almost always the same regardless of the temperature of the environment. Warm-blooded animals use food as "fuel" to produce heat.

abdomen 12
acacia ant 14
adder 137
alligator gar 172
amber 101
ambush bug 34
amphibians 150–7
anaconda 134
anglerfish 177, 178
antennae 12
ant lion 112
ant mimic spider 74
ants 12–19
aphid 34
aquatic leech 106
arachnids 66, 72
arachnophobia 72
archerfish 172
armored ground cricket 46
army ant 15, 16
arrow crab 168
asp viper 138
axolotl 152

bark scorpion 68
basilisk lizard 124, 125
beaded lizard 131
bearded dragon 124
bedbug 32, 34
bee assassin bug 35
bee-killer wasp 98
bees 96–103
beetles 20–31
bird-eating spider 74
black fly 54
black mamba 141
black-necked spitting cobra 141
black widow spider 75
blister beetle 22
bluebottle 54
blue-ringed octopus 166, 167
boa 145
bobbit worm 106

body louse 93
bolas spider 75
bombardier beetle 22
boomslang 140
botfly 54
box jellyfish 173
brown recluse spider 76
brown snake 135
Budgett's frog 154
bug 32–41
bulldog ant 14
bullet ant 14
bullfrog 152, 153
bush cricket 51
bushmaster 135
bush viper 144
butterfly bug 35

camouflage 39, 44, 48
cane toad 155
cannibal spider 83
caterpillars 60–3
cave spider 76
centipede 113
cephalopod 166
cephalothorax 66, 165
chagas bug 35
chameleon 122, 123
chigger flea 93
chigger mite 92
chordotonal organs 16
chuckwalla 124
cicada 36
cicada-killer wasp 96, 98
click beetle 23
cobra 134, 146
cockroach 44–51
coelacanth 173
cold-blooded 120
Colorado beetle 23
common green tiger beetle 30
common house spider 80
common scorpion fly 117

common wasp 98
cone shell 162
conger eel 176
coral snake 138
cottonmouth snake 148
crabs 168, 169
crab spider 77, 78
creepy crawlies 110–17
crickets 44–51
crown-of-thorns starfish 173
crustaceans 160–9
cuckoo spit 40
cuckoo wasp 99
cuttlefish 164

damsel bug 36
dance fly 55, 56
darner 115
dart frog 156
death adder 137
death's-head hawk moth 62
death stalker scorpion 68
deerfly 55
desert horned viper 149
desert locust 46
devil's coach horse 27
dewdrop spider 77
diamondback rattlesnake 137
diving beetle 26
dog whelk 162
dragonfish 179
dragonfly 115
driver ant 15
dry-wood termite 19
dung beetle 23
dust mite 92
dwarf spider 77

eagle ray 187
earwig 112
eel 170, 174, 176
egg-eating snake 140
electric eel 174

electric ray 176
elegant grasshopper 48
elephant beetle 24, 25
emperor scorpion 68, 69
exoskeleton 165
eyelash viper 136
eyespot 39

feelers 12
fer-de-lance 140
fierce snake 145
fire-bellied toad 154
firefish 179
firefly 36, 37
fireworm 106
fleas 90–3
flies 52–9
Florida walking stick 48
flying lizard 126
fog-basking beetle 24
fossils 154
frilled lizard 126
frogfish 177
froghopper 40
frogs 152–7
fungus bug 38
funnel-web spider 81, 86

Gaboon viper 149
gadfly 55
gecko 123
German cockroach 47
giraffe beetle 24
glow fly 37
glowworm 37
golden tree snake 135
Goliath beetle 26
grasshopper 46, 48
gray slug 107
great silver beetle 26
green anole 131
green lynx spider 81
green mamba 146, 147

green tiger beetle 30
green tree python 142
ground beetle 29
ground chameleon 122
ground cricket 46
gulper eel 170, 174, 175

hagfish 170, 177
hard tick 92
harlequin beetle 27, 28
harlequin shrimp 164, 165
harvester ant 15
harvestman 115
hatchetfish 170, 174
hawker dragonfly 115
head lice 90, 93
Hercules beetle 27
hermaphrodites 104
hermit crab 168
hickory horned devil 62
hissing cockroach 49
honeybee 96, 98
honeypot ant 17, 18
horned orb weaver 79
horned toad 127, 154
hornet 99, 100
horsefly 55
horseshoe crab 169
house spider 80
hoverfly 57
huntsman spider 80

ichneumon wasp 101
iguana 122, 126
imitation 39
invertebrates 110

Jackson's chameleon 122
jellyfish 173, 179, 183, 184
Jesus lizard 124
jockey spider 74
jumping spider 80
jumping viper 144

Index

killer bee 101
king baboon spider 84
king cobra 134
kissing bug 35

lacewing 112
lamprey 186
lancehead snake 140
land leech 107
lantern bug 38, 39
leaf insect 115, 116
leaf-tailed gecko 123
leafy sea dragon 179
leeches 104–9
lepidoptera 60
lice 57, 90–3
lightning bug 37
lionfish 179
lion's mane jellyfish 179
lizards 120–31
lobster 163
lobster moth 63
Loch Ness Monster 180
longhorn beetle 22
long-nosed tree snake 148
lungfish 172
lynx spider 80, 81

MacLeay's specter 49, 50
maggots 54
malarial mosquito 57, 59
mamba 146, 147
mammals 120
mandibles 32
mangrove snake 146
mantella frog 155
mantises 44–51
mantis shrimp 162
marine iguana 126
Massasauga rattlesnake 149
metamorphosis 157
millipede 113, 114
mite 90–3

mole cricket 49
mollusks 160–9
monitor lizard 127, 128, 129
monkfish 178
mosquito 57, 59
moths 60–3
mouse spider 81
mudskipper 180, 181

nautilus 166
Nile monitor 127, 128
nits 93

oarfish 180
octopus 166, 167
ogre-faced spider 81, 82
old world scorpion 70
opalescent squid 166
orb spider 79
ornate horned frog 155
ornate mantis 51

paper wasp 101
paradoxical frog 156, 157
parasites 54, 90
piranha fish 182
pirate spider 83
pistol shrimp 163
pit viper 144
plague flea 93
poison-dart frog 156
pond skater 38
porcupine fish 182
Portia spider 83
Portuguese man-of-war 183, 184
praying mantis 51
proboscis 32
puff adder 134
puffer fish 182
purse-web spider 83
puss moth 63
python 132, 136

Queen Alexandra's birdwing butterfly 62

raft spider 79
rattlesnake 137, 149
redback spider 74
red-bellied black snake 145
red crab 168
red-kneed spider 84, 85
regal horned lizard 127
rhinoceros-horned viper 138, 139
ringhal 148
robber crab 169
robber fly 58
rolling wasp 102
rove beetle 27

saber-tooth ground beetle 29
sac spider 89
salamander 152
Salvador's monitor 129
sandfish skink 129
savanna monitor 129
sawfish 182, 183
saw-scaled viper 137
Sawyer beetle 29
scorpion fish 183
scorpion fly 117
scorpions 66–71
scorpling 71
screwworm fly 58
sea anemone 185
sea creatures 170–89
sea cucumber 185
sea horse 179, 185
sea krait 142, 143
sea lamprey 186
sea nettle 185
sea robin 186
sea slug 164
sea urchin 186
sexton beetle 29

shingleback skink 123
shrimp 162, 163, 164
silk 74
silver beetle 26
silverfish 110, 117
skink 123, 129
skunk beetle 30
slave-making ant 17
sleeping sickness 58
slipper lobster 163
slugs 104–9
snake charmers 144
snakes 132–49
social insects 12
sphenodont 131
spider crab 169
spider-hunting wasp 102
spiderling 74
spiders 72–89
spider silk 74
spiny lobster 163
spitting cobra 141
spitting spider 84
spittle bug 40
squid 166
stag beetle 30, 31
starfish 173, 176
stargazer 187
stick insect 44
stinkbug 40
stonefish 187
stylet 32
sunfish 182
sun-gazer lizard 130
Suriname toad 156
Sydney funnel-web spider 86

tadpole 150
taipan 145
tapeworm 108, 109
tarantula 84, 85
tarantula hawk wasp 102, 103
termites 12–19

thick-tailed scorpion 70, 71
thorax 12
thorny devil 130
ticks 90–3
tigerfish 188
tiger moth 62
tiger snake 142
tiger spider 86
toad 154, 155, 156
toad bug 40
toadfish 188
toe biter 41
trapdoor spider 87, 88
treehopper 41
tree python 142
tree snake 148
triggerfish 188
tsetse fly 58
tuatara 131
turkeyfish 179
twig snake 136

velvet worm 108
vine snake 141
viper 136, 137, 138, 139, 144, 149
viperfish 189

wandering spider 75, 76
warm-blooded 120
wasps 96–103
water spider 87
weaver ant 19
weaverfish 189
weta 48
white ant 12
white-tailed spider 87
wolffish 189
wolf spider 89
wood louse spider 89
worms 104–9

yellow fat-tailed scorpion 70
yellow sac spider 89

Bullet Ant

Harvester Ant

Dung Beetle

Weaver Ant

Honeypot Ant

Blister Beetle

Elephant Beetle

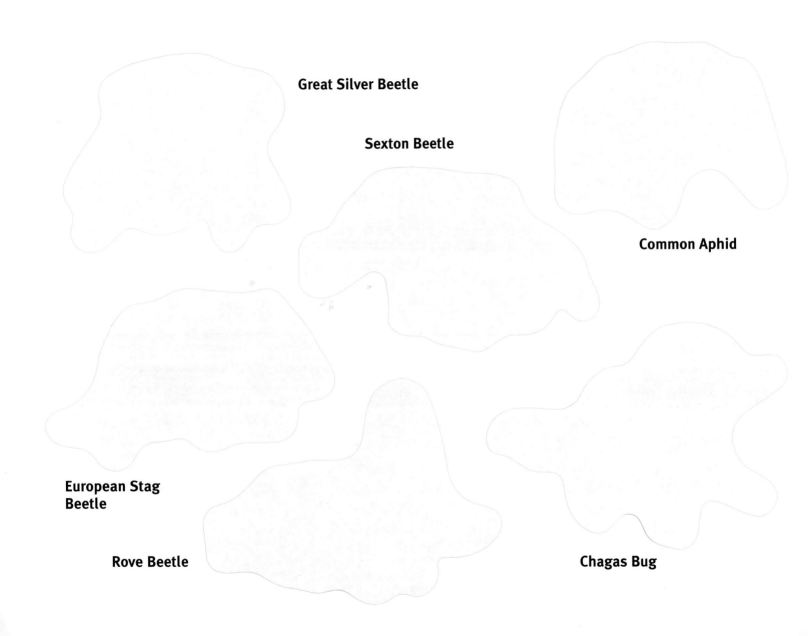

Great Silver Beetle

Sexton Beetle

Common Aphid

European Stag
Beetle

Rove Beetle

Chagas Bug

Firefly

Lantern Bug

Elegant Grasshopper

Stinkbug

German Cockroach

Treehopper

Botfly

Mole Cricket

Hoverfly

Horsefly

Tsetse Fly

Ornate Mantis

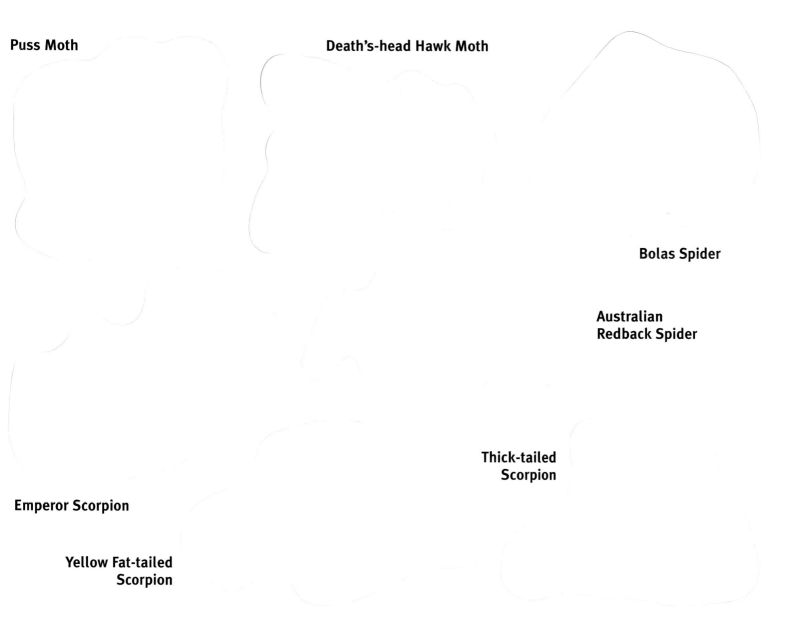

Puss Moth

Death's-head Hawk Moth

Bolas Spider

Australian
Redback Spider

Thick-tailed
Scorpion

Emperor Scorpion

Yellow Fat-tailed
Scorpion

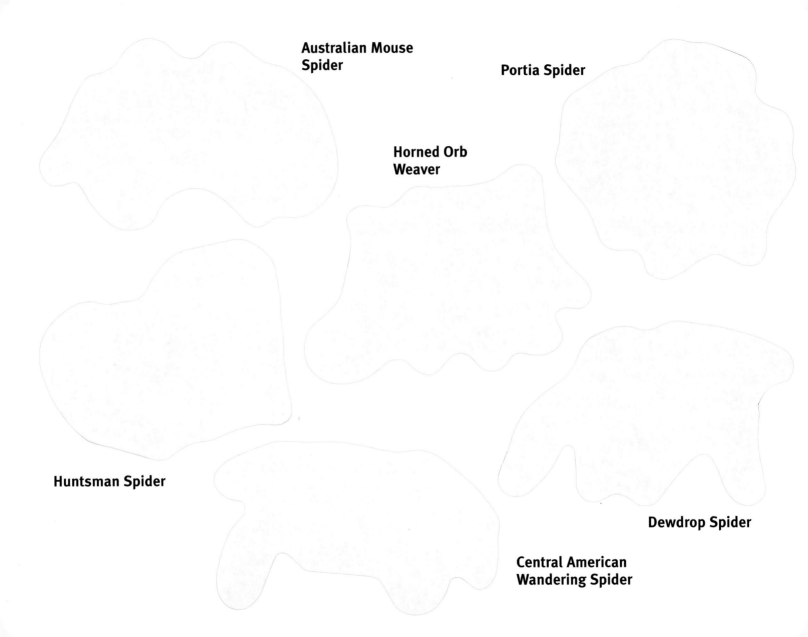

Australian Mouse Spider

Portia Spider

Horned Orb Weaver

Huntsman Spider

Dewdrop Spider

Central American Wandering Spider

Chigger Flea

Trapdoor Spider

Indian Tiger
Spider

Chigger Mite

Wood Louse Spider

Mexican Red-kneed
Spider

Bee-killer Wasp

Aquatic Leech

European Hornet

Killer Bee

Paper Wasp

Tarantula Hawk Wasp

Land Leech

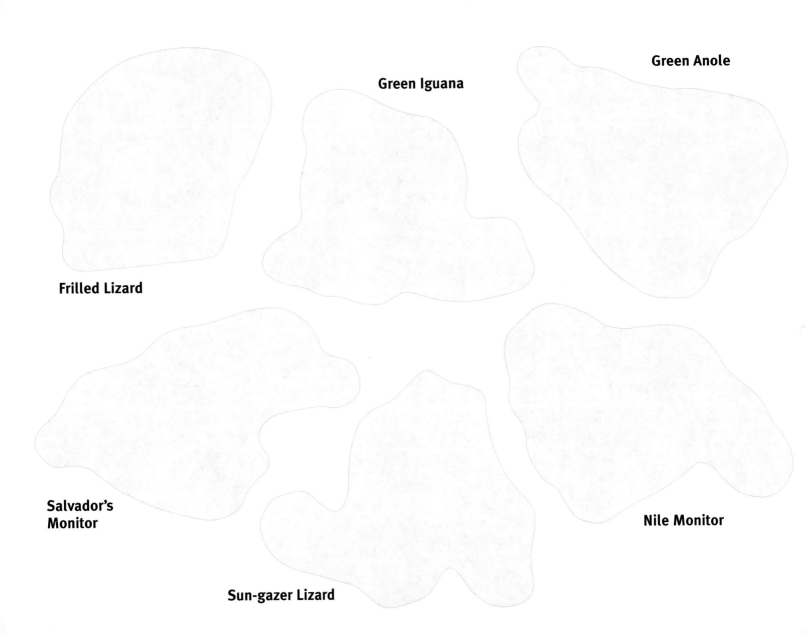

Green Iguana

Green Anole

Frilled Lizard

Salvador's Monitor

Sun-gazer Lizard

Nile Monitor

Death Adder

Anaconda

Black Mamba

Brown Snake

Rhinoceros-
horned Viper

African Twig
Snake

Boomslang

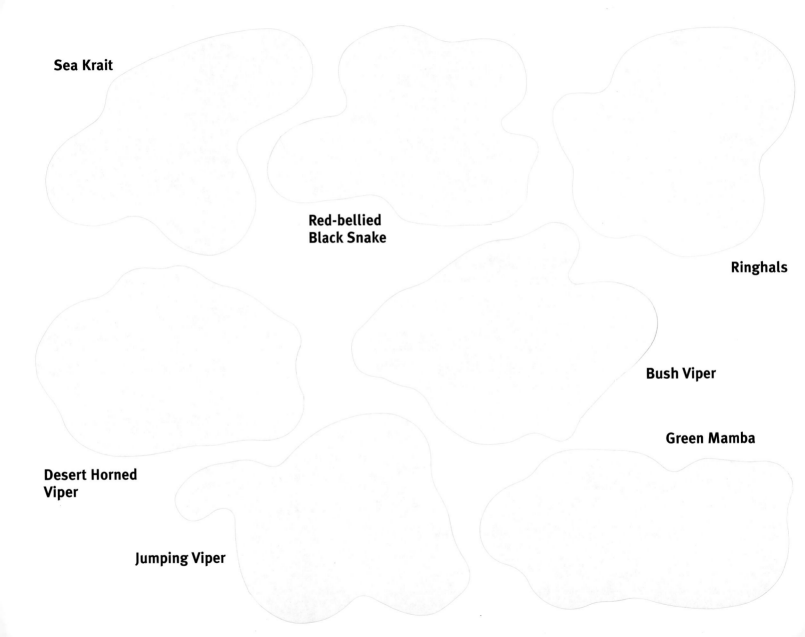

Sea Krait

Red-bellied
Black Snake

Ringhals

Bush Viper

Green Mamba

Desert Horned
Viper

Jumping Viper

African Bullfrog

Fire-bellied
Toad

Spiny Lobster

Paradoxical
Frog

Cane Toad

Dog Whelk

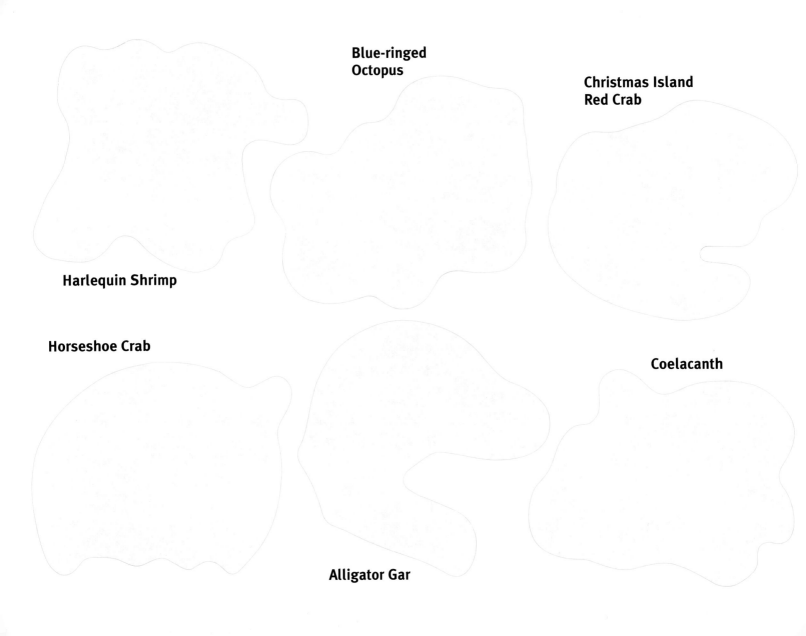

Blue-ringed Octopus

Christmas Island Red Crab

Harlequin Shrimp

Horseshoe Crab

Coelacanth

Alligator Gar

Deep-sea
Gulper Eel

Ocean Sunfish

Anglerfish

Leafy Sea
Dragon

European
Conger Eel

Mudskipper

Sea Robin

Stonefish

**Portuguese
Man-of-War**

Weaverfish

Sea Horse

Triggerfish

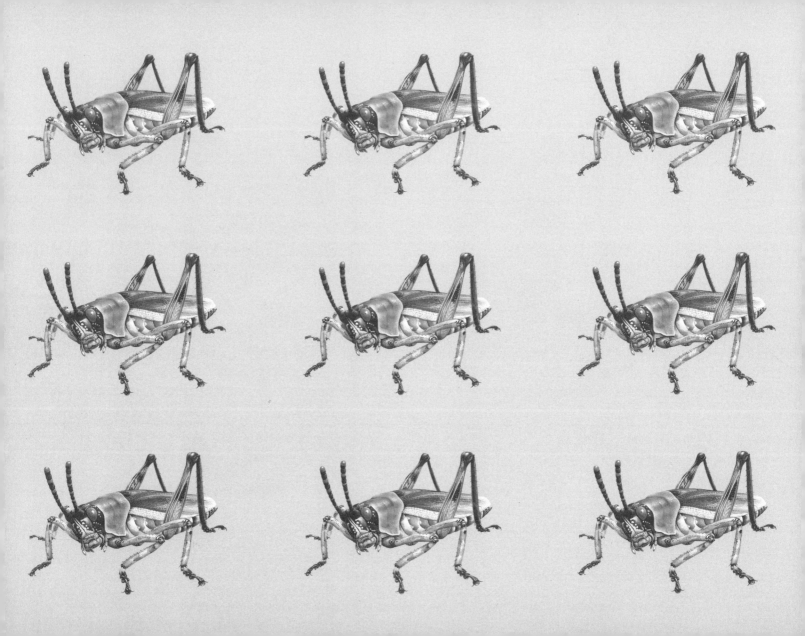